Successful Career Management

A Guide for Organisations, Leaders and Individuals

Stuart McAdam

Thorogood Publishing Ltd
10-12 Rivington Street
London EC2A 3DU
Telephone: 020 7749 4748

Email: info@thorogoodpublishing.co.uk
Web: www.thorogoodpublishing.co.uk

A CIP catalogue record for this book is available
from the British Library.

ISBN: (10) 1854188186 (13) 9781854188182

Printed and bound in Great Britain by
Marston Book Services Limited, Oxfordshire

Table of Contents

Acknowledgements

Many people have helped to get this book into print, some without realising it! Special thanks are due to:

Anthony Wills, Emma Gant, Claudia Knüsel, Marie Jose Platzer, Tim Johnson, Laura Miles, Dan Miles, Michael Moran, Diana Wright, David Robertson, Melanie Jones, Tracey Gleed, Keith Boyfield, John Engestrom, Dan Zegibe, Celia Baxter, Melanie Robertson, Clara Geary, Matthew Andews, Oliver Hibbert, Anne Williams, John Hatton, Angus Frew, Malcolm Gregory, Matthew K McCreight, Richard Parker, Adrian Furnham, Justin Phillimore, Alison Vickers, Steve Nuttall, Laura Dale Williams, and Sophie Huxtable.

About the author

Stuart McAdam has occupied a variety of senior roles during his career, necessitating strategic understanding, operational management skills and a pragmatic, hands-on approach to delivering effective, lasting change.

He worked for the local government employers organisation, LACSAB (Local Authorities' Conditions of Service Advisory Board) as a Principal Officer in one of the national pay bargaining teams and subsequently for the Confederation of British Industry focusing on effective employee communications and involvement. He was a Principal Consultant at KPMG and then Group HR Director at M&G Reinsurance and became the Executive Board Member responsible for Global HR at Swiss Re Life & Health when M&G Re was acquired. He was subsequently Global HR Director at GE SeaCo, the container leasing business. He has worked as an executive search consultant, focusing on Risk and Actuarial needs and was a Lecturer in Management Studies at Nene College, Northampton.

Stuart attended Marling School, Stroud and read International Politics at Lancaster University, subsequently gaining an MA in War Studies from Kings College London and an MBA from Bradford University. He is a licensed Master NLP Practitioner and trained as an executive coach at the School of Coaching and The Tavistock Institute. He is a registered user of a number of psychometric tools including the Hogan inventories. He is a

Chartered FCIPD, FRSA and a Member of the Association for Coaching.

He has contributed articles to a variety of journals and spoken at a number of conferences. He co-wrote *"Be Your Own Management Consultant"* (FT Pitman), along with a chapter on the same theme for the *"FT Handbook of Management"*. He contributed a chapter on Talent as part of the Henry Stewart Management series and his book, *"Executive Coaching"* (Thorogood Publishing), recently became available in Polish as well as English.

Stuart is Principal Consultant at New Futures Consulting focusing on executive coaching, talent and career management and the effective management of change.

New Futures Consulting

New Futures Consulting offers solutions to corporate and personal challenges.

The economic upheavals of the opening decades of the 21st century have necessitated new perspectives on corporate strategy and career choices. We live in an environment characterised by increasingly rapid change, which brings with it both uncertainty and opportunity. In such circumstances, organisations and individuals may unconsciously revert to unproductive patterns of behaviour. This may cause a much heralded transformation to emerge instead as a re-formation, delivering significantly less benefit than expected or required. New Futures Consulting helps organisations and individuals recognise, understand and productively mitigate these behaviours, paving the ground for sustainable, successful change.

As organisations restructure, upsize and downsize, the need to retain - and continue to attract - talent remains paramount. New Futures Consulting advises on talent and career management, assessing and benchmarking talent for organisations undergoing change; and support re-energising employee engagement and performance management processes. The role of the line manager as talent spotter and coach has been significantly underestimated; we run small group training in executive coaching skills for line managers to address these issues.

Rapid change, high levels of pressure or sudden professional or personal reversals can also derail individuals. The need to assimilate speedily to the culture of a new organisation also presents fresh demands. Our individually tailored executive coaching programmes address these needs.

Preface

"If you want a happy ending, it just depends on where you close the book."

Orson Welles

Some years ago, as a newly appointed Group Human Resources Director, I espoused the notion of the importance of "employability" for our workforce. Whereas today "employability" has far wider currency, at this time the issue of what an individual might need to do in terms of gaining experience and skills to enhance their suitability for future roles was less well understood. On reflection I may have pushed the significance of employability with too much enthusiasm, since the response to this notion was not always positive. In part this arose from a culture in which "the Company" rather than the individual held prime accountability for career development; and the notion of personal ownership, particularly in a business with a high proportion of long-serving staff and a paternalistic culture, was no doubt disconcerting. This was also an organisation which had not experienced large-scale change and, as a consequence, the tools and processes needed to underpin a shift towards more personal ownership were not – yet – in position. An additional burden that some people paradoxically carried was their concern that dispassionately reviewing their career options was somehow "disloyal" to the current employer. Just as some have imposter syndrome, feeling themselves to be unworthy in their current role, so might others feel it to be "unworthy" to look elsewhere. This is well illustrated by the comment of an individual who took some time to decide to make a career move: "I am fairly resistant to change and very reluctant to disappoint, (which) has meant I have often stayed in a role or organisation for a little longer than I necessarily should have."

Over the years I have reflected on this dilemma and today see an even greater need for individuals to have their own means of determining whether it's better to move on or stay. "What's the **'Return on Me (ROM)'** this organisation may be able to provide?" is a question we should all ask ourselves.

A recent report by the Chartered Institute of Personnel and Development exemplifies the importance of understanding your career options and reported in 2013 that 20% of employees say they would be looking for a new job in the next 12 months. The Institute (CIPD "Megatrends, 2013) questions whether the "current state of the labour market is simply encouraging a lot of employees to 'sit tight' in their jobs until the economy recovers or whether we have seen a shift to a labour market that is less dynamic". In either case, the rationale for moving on or staying put requires careful consideration.

I see the need to differentiate between talent management and career management: the former being a corporate activity and potentially done **to** employees rather than **with** them; the latter individually focused but frequently lacking sufficient personal ownership and understanding to deliver the required outcome. As an individual contemplating their own career ambitions told me: "It may be important to the organisation to have the right number of talented people, but to me it's potentially my one and only career opportunity." This is particularly important in today's environment, where moving on may be more difficult than in the past. Leveraging the opportunities available – but untapped – in your current organisation is therefore worth serious consideration. That said, "downsizing" and restructuring are very much a fact of life, so the option of staying put may prove illusory. Consequently it is best to be prepared; passively waiting for outplacement to help you re-enter the labour market is a very risky approach.

As my estimable history master Mr Pankhurst drummed into me, it is risky to generalise on anything. And by the time you read this book there may well have been shifts on many levels – organisational, personal, political and economic. Indeed, as I am writing, the IMF is sounding alarm bells about the slowing growth of the BRIC (Brazil, Russia, India and China) along with other emerging economies and the condition of the Portuguese finances. Riding the change curve is all about knowing where you are now, and anticipating where change may take you – and whether this is where you wish to be taken! Having the tools, energy and confidence to take personal ownership of your career management and destiny is fundamental. This can of course be potentially very uncomfortable whatever your job.

For leadership teams a change such as a takeover, IPO, M&A, or restructuring can bring big rewards and is often seen as intrinsically rewarding in the shape of experience. As a CFO in a business recently acquired by a North American parent observed: "Things are very different on many levels; the downs I experience are significant but so is the upside in opening up new career opportunities both as a leader and an individual."

But what of those of us who are not in the leadership team? Those on the top deck generally have some idea of the direction of travel and a smoother journey. If you are on the lower deck or in the engine room the ride is bumpier with little sense of what's coming next. Good organisations recognise this and up their game in the shape of frequent two-way communication to increase awareness of the need for change whether to tackle challenges such as market shifts or to increase organisational competitiveness.

The people who emerge with an understanding of what they need to do to manage their careers will be those who are prepared to invest the time in better understanding themselves and how best to leverage their unique skills. It is not surprising that there has been a mini boom in the self-help arena with many books offering ideas on self-employment, and providing techniques for accelerating your approach to getting the job of your dreams. This book is not about making you someone you are not; rather it will support making you the individual you have the potential to be.

For this to happen it's important to recognise the trade-offs that may be required to achieve the outcome you desire. This requires an understanding of both the short-term consequences of your actions and their longer-term impact. Career planning is not about a continually upward trajectory; reverses can and do occur. Neither is there a foolproof formula for getting it right. The premise underpinning this book is that a structured approach which supports both flexibility and reflection adds value.

This book will have relevance to someone in your life: yourself, neighbour, colleague, children or parents whether as bosses, employees, job seekers, mentors or someone who's not sure how best to help someone make sense of the labour market. We cover a wide range of issues and, for many people, their instinctive reaction to the suggestion from an outsider that a variety of new actions are now required can be at best lukewarm. Indeed sometimes resistance is disguised by lukewarm approval. There is no compulsion to take any of the actions suggested in this book; however, the suggestions are based on what has worked for others and will support your desire to actively manage your own career.

It may seem strange to start by looking back, but here are the observations of a number of individuals at different stages in their careers on what they have learned and maybe could have done a little differently during their own career journey:

- "Looking back, I could have taken a few more chances, moved around a bit more – I got a bit 'comfortable' in some jobs and could have pushed myself harder. In particular it was the circumstances, rather than drive, which led me into self-employment – I wish I had been braver and more ambitious in my 30s. So the learning would be: if you think you can, then go for it, because you may not get another chance. Also keep things in proportion so you don't get so caught up in work that you lose sight of the rest of your life."

- "Many career opportunities are about luck, being in the right place at the right time. We can do things to improve opportunities and prospects, but sometimes we can't."

- "I could have worked harder in developing a network within the larger companies I was employed by. Promotional opportunities are not only a function of performance in larger firms but equally so a function of having internal promoters; I could have done that more effectively."

- "My most significant learning experiences have been that I can really accomplish just about anything I set my mind to if I am willing to commit the resources to achieving it. I also feel self-cultivation (continued growth) of body, mind and spirit is imperative to accomplish goals and stay sane."

- "I should have got moving earlier in my career (early 20s not 30s) on real skill development and (got myself) earlier access to a mentor/role model."

- "I think that while we are able to learn from mistakes, dwelling on the past and seeing them as such does no good. If I had done things differently then I might not be faced with the opportunities I have now. I am very happy, which is the most important thing to me. That being said, I am constantly looking to do well and feel challenged. If I start to feel unhappy or unchallenged in a role I will start to do something about it. I feel happy with most of the decisions I have made to date and as a result have grown in confidence."

The book uses the framework illustrated below to guide the reader to more ownership of their career, exploring the "what, why, and how" of career management.

The **Steps** are the stages we all go through in developing our careers, whether moving on or staying put; this is a linear journey although usually one with a few diversions and dead ends. Of the Steps, the mapping phase is the one which drives everything else. Although we all go through these stages a word of caution is necessary, since the time spent on each stage will vary significantly depending on the circumstances each of us face. But also, when feeling pressured to take action and move on, we may just do that. Skimming one or more steps without fully understanding their significance is detrimental to fulfilling your career goals.

Effective **Self-Management** is what you need to be able to do to proactively manage your own career journey. An important characteristic is the capacity to make the right connections both literally with those who can help you and personally by better understanding yourself and your aspirations. These character-istics embrace:

- The capacity to be effectively networked to the labour market and to those people who may be able to help you.

- Investing time to better understand oneself before making sense of the wider environment.

- The ability to take a balanced approach to career manage-ment which recognises that focus combined with desire is a powerful combination, but one without the other leads to a distorted view of what's possible.

The **Processes** include a range of activities and support which are of use at various points during your own career journey. As we shall see, their usefulness depends on the curiosity and per-sistence of the recipient as much as the expertise of the provider. They include the importance of seeking – and using – feedback along with the need to understand your own organ-isation's performance review processes. Depending on your circumstances, outplacement, executive coaching and mentor-ing may have a role to play. And at the core of this book is something that will probably surprise many readers – "My Big Fat CV" (MBFCV). The power of an effective CV is often dra-matically reduced by the desire to get on with the process of finding a new job as quickly as possible, without understanding how much a poorly composed CV will weaken your prospects of getting an interview let alone securing a new job.

The steps	Self-Management	Processes
Mapping	Balancing Focus & Desire	Feedback and the Performance Review
Planning		
Exploring	Insight	Outplacement, Executive Coaching and Mentoring
Demonstrating Competence		
Arriving & Delivering	Connecting	My Big Fat CV
Consolidating & Reviewing		

The Takeaway

During the research for this book, many of those I spoke to commented that a number of the themes we were exploring had prompted them to address some issues in a new way: "I'm not sure I've thought about my career choices in this way before" was a frequent response. Sometimes we have no choice but to respond to changes; this book can give you the impetus to better understand yourself and the labour market and thereby take a more proactive approach. So, taking on board the spirit of the quotation at the start of this Preface, please do keep turning the pages...

Chapter One
Putting Career Management in Context

"The single biggest problem in communication is the illusion that it has taken place."

George Bernard Shaw

This book focuses on career management from both a corporate and individual perspective. Organisations can do more to fully engage with their people; and all of us need to be open to how best to manage our own careers if we are to fulfil our own ambitions against a backdrop of continuing worldwide economic uncertainty. Very few books are of themselves transformational; however, the actions that are subsequently taken by the reader may be. Hopefully this book will present some new ways of examining situations and opportunities from a different perspective. The aim is to contribute to the process of making sense of a highly competitive labour market not by providing instant solutions but through processes for self-analysis and individual and corporate reflection.

The focus is therefore upon how individuals may best develop their own approach to getting the best return on oneself and also examines how organisations can proactively embrace the concept of **ROM** to better engage with their people. Supervisors and line managers are frequently ignored as the links in the process and the opportunity to do more to get them involved is explored in Chapter Eleven.

The on-going uncertainty created by what is the world's first genuinely global recession has implications at every level and location, from macroeconomic forecasting by the World Bank to the price of onions in India. It is clear that the duration and impact of the "crash" is going to be greater and longer lasting than anticipated only a couple of years ago. The interconnectedness of the global village has delivered considerable benefits, but the corrosive impact of "instant" communication upon a world economy still seeking the confidence to rebuild itself is producing divergence rather than convergence at many levels.

This does not mean that career opportunities have disappeared, or that all organisations are in permanent lay-off mode. But making sense of a fast-moving puzzle, with often contradictory outcomes, does require patience and resilience. These days both individuals and organisations are on a more or less constant journey of change. Moreover it's a journey where it is not always possible to anticipate what will happen along the way. We have entered an era of dilemma and paradox – a form of "Rubik's cube" of competing challenges and potential uncertainties. This is exemplified by those organisations which can appear bipolar as they stretch to both attract and retain talent whilst also having to contemplate plant closures, cost cutting and restructuring as they face up to new market challenges. Those organisations likely to confront and effectively manage these competing challenges are those making significantly greater use of active employee engagement strategies and processes.

The bigger picture

Add climate change, the Arab Spring and the potential capacity of rogue states to derail a fragile global recovery and the frail condition of the Eurozone economies to the recipe, and it is easy to understand why it is a necessity to regularly recalibrate personal expectations against what is possible. This does not mean saying goodbye to ambition, quite the contrary. However, without a sense of where you are now it is impossible to measure progress and to reset objectives.

This book does not pretend to have the answers to these geopolitical problems, nor can it claim to have a universal answer to the need to re-energise the global economy. However, today's environment necessitates, at the very least, individuals and organisations reviewing the way in which careers and talent are managed.

Whilst the global economy may have the resilience to recover, established strategic panaceas such as downsizing, outsourcing and retrenchment may not work in the face of the challenges that the future holds. And remember that each and every time a downsizing occurs, a proportion of the "survivors" who remain with the organisation will actively contemplate a move to a potentially safer environment. "Safer" can mean a search for greater security but it may also embrace an industry or sector that is in growth or an organisation that looks a better bet for career development or the desire for a change in working environment and personal lifestyle.

The leaders who will be running successful organisations in the future are those who recognise that a different approach is needed, based upon systematically developing a clearer view of what the future may hold and actively managing the transition to the new world. The "war for talent" – attracting, developing and retaining good people – remains a challenge, even in times of duress. Attracting and retaining the "right" talent is an important element in ensuring organisational survival. The pay-off for the organisation in getting this right is considerable, including the use of robust career management processes to develop the bench strength of next generation leadership contenders. This does not mean cloning or never "letting go" of able people. Good leavers are good for business; so too are those who are able to take a divergent perspective on business needs. The process of clarifying who has the "right stuff" requires a culture which encourages transparent discussions on career potential. It necessitates the acknowledgement that convergent and divergent perceptions are required.

Are new competencies required to master a significantly different business landscape? Is talent management aligned to business strategy? Is the CEO's involvement visible and consistent? Where does talent management sit in the HR hierarchy? And are succession and performance management processes congruent with a common language to articulate what's wanted?

However, organisations and those leading them can, and often do, revert to unproductive patterns of behaviour when under pressure. Managing the present without compromising the future is particularly relevant in the context of managing talent, with short-term thinking potentially jeopardising future organisational capability and capacity. The era of being sent on a training course as a gift or to lessen the blow of failed promotion, or to show someone they were important to the organisation is, hopefully, long gone. A key issue for any organisation during any downturn is the need to balance the competing needs of taking appropriate measures to maintain the integrity of the organisation as a going concern **and** taking the necessary action to ensure the enterprise is fit to compete as the downturn ends and as new opportunities emerge. Investing in talent management is a critical part of this process and career management can provide the means for making this process of greater relevance to individuals.

The phrase "precarious employment" is more widely used these days with some assessments suggesting that about one in ten of the UK's workforce may be in this position.

Those employed – but not "fully employed" – will sit in this category, and whilst some are very content with a less than full-time role others would no doubt really like to get themselves back into a full employment mode. The part-time route may have attractions for both employee and employer potentially providing greater flexibility for both.

There is also the impact of the so-called "hourglass" economy to consider with opportunities increasing at the high and low skill ends of the labour market and opportunities in the middle becoming squeezed. Certainly the notion of the lifetime career is clearly being challenged at the same time as people are contemplating the need to work longer with the number of people in employment in the UK aged 65 or over topping one million for the first time in 2013. The charity Age UK has welcomed the increase but noted that those who remain in the labour market tend to have stayed in a job or have become self-employed whereas those trying to find a job again after redundancy or a spell as a carer were likely to face barriers to employment.

Older workers are needed because current forecasting suggests there will be 13.5 million vacancies in the next ten years, but only seven million people will leave school and college during the same period. However, a newspaper headline accentuates the consequential impact of this rise in older workers remaining in employment: "Young workers fear later retirement blocks career prospects" (*Financial Times*, June 30 2013). The story focused on a survey of 1,500 people by KPMG (May 2013) which suggested the possibility of intergenerational conflict in the workplace with 46% of respondents agreeing with the proposition that older members of staff should retire so that younger workers could have a genuine chance of promotion. It was noted that "six years of economic stagnation have meant that many are holding onto their jobs".

However, as with most of the issues and ideas reviewed in this book, it is risky to generalise. A lifetime career in a sector or large organisation is still possible. But – and it's a big but – career management in what is an uncertain environment, calls for a far more sophisticated approach than in the past and your own ambitions need recalibration on a regular basis. For the individual the challenge is "how do I engage with my organisation and/or the employment market, in a way that gives me more control over my current and future career path?"

Whatever the scenario, a lack of self-awareness can derail this process and this book will enable you to test out your feelings and thinking from a range of perspectives. Perspectives are important; as the owner/manager of your own career and brand, how much of yourself do you generally see? And how often do you proactively seek feedback on your approach and prospects? Without this capacity to take a helicopter view of yourself – and inviting others' observations as part of the process – you are less likely to make sense of the environment in which you are trying to shape your career.

And where will jobs of the future come from along with the people with the skills to perform them? On the macro level there are always indications in the shape of government funding for particular projects such as infrastructure. The most recent (2013) data on applications for university places in the

UK show the biggest increases over the previous year coming in computer sciences and engineering; and social services, arts and languages recording the biggest fall.

Depending on sector, geography and market conditions it is always good to get a sense of where your organisation sees the condition of its own talent pipeline. Spikes in demand can and do create the opportunity to make a move. The European insurance industry has experienced both demand and shortages as the Solvency II Directive necessitated significant hiring by insurers and consultancies, increasing salaries and attracting individuals to contract roles.

The challenge of "going where the future is" has taken on a significant trans-border dimension which was illustrated in June 2013 by the BBC's Gavin Hewitt. He reported that: "For many, Germany is the land of opportunity and jobs. In 2012, 45,000 Italians moved to Germany. The Spanish were not far behind, with 37,000 heading in the same direction; 35,000 Greeks also left for Germany. Germany needs these migrants. The Association of German Engineers says it wants 70,000 engineers immediately. When scientists and IT specialists are included, the figure goes up to 200,000." He noted that to help this need to be fulfilled, Germany is investing one billion euros (£848m; $1.3bn) in funding apprenticeships for young people in places like Spain and Portugal to support their search for work in Germany.

In a thoughtful piece in *"The Guardian"*, Sonia Sodha observed that: "The question savvy 18-year-olds will increasingly ask is, 'What will my degree be worth?' Plenty of graduates find themselves in "graduate" jobs that wouldn't have required a degree ten years ago...some jobs will always require an academic degree. But there are some...where employers might be better off training young people on the job on an apprenticeship wage." So **ROM** may now be playing a role at this early stage as well.

Organisations still need to hang onto their best people and it seems to me that in parallel with "precarious employment" another phenomenon has emerged, "vicarious employee engagement", whereby the organisation and its leadership espouse the benefits of employee engagement but are in reality one step away from truly active employee engagement. These organisations are ostensibly doing the right things, but not delivering or getting what they really want; reacting to, rather than anticipating opportunities and challenges for upskilling their workforce and proactively encouraging diversity.

Talent provides a significant source of differential advantage to organisations and, no matter how sophisticated the processes to manage it, good people can still be ignored or forgotten. The question organisations should repeatedly ask themselves is: "How do we engage with our people and potential hires so that they are motivated to give us their best and realise their true potential?" Those who lead organisations are people too; putting yourself in the position of your workforce is the first step toward active employee engagement.

Engagement in organisations must be two way. Leaders, leadership teams and line managers all need to be credible and trusted if they are to develop a genuine sense of shared destiny and interconnectedness. Equally, employees need to understand how to engage with their organisations, with personal career management having the potential to support their efforts to do so. Underpinning this is the need to be mindful of your own **ROM**; how you may best leverage yourself to get the career move you need. Whilst organisations quite rightly place emphasis on measuring their return on investment, the assessment of the returns derived from interventions such as learning and development can prove to be vexatious.

The Takeaway

Making sense of the labour market is more complex than in the past; choices may be fewer and the consequences of your actions greater. What does your next job need to deliver in terms of your own **ROM**?

Chapter Two
The Individual Perspective – Key Elements

"Being sacked is a gift."

John Lloyd, BBC Desert Island Discs, 2012

Over the last five years there have been fundamental changes to the established notion of careers. The current state of the global economy and resulting slowdown in growth is creating major challenges for individuals and organisations. For career professionals the slowdown has important implications for their anticipated career trajectory; it is also leading many individuals and their families to review what they really want from their working lives. A key aspect is the need to adopt a proactive approach to managing your own career – both within the current organisation and, potentially, elsewhere. This chapter provides an overview of the Steps along which all career journeys progress and the role of personal preferences in how we tackle them.

The implications of a global slowdown in economic activity are considerable. In many markets the immediate impact is fewer jobs for an increasing pool of job seekers. Perversely, as ever in times of trouble, able people seek control of their own careers presenting their current employer with the challenge of retaining scarce talent. The notion of always looking outside one's current employer for a new job needs rethinking; it may be much more useful to leverage your skills in an environment you know; albeit one in which your true worth may not yet be fully appreciated.

These days you need to be much more nimble and resilient than in the past to identify and exploit opportunities. Those in work, looking for their next job or facing retirement or redundancy are focusing more on what they need to do to get what they want from an increasingly fractured employment market. New graduates ask "How long will it take me to find a real job?" and potential pensioners ask "How long do I need to keep working?" These are concerns which are not exclusive to those in so-called advanced economies; the BRIC economies have their challenges too. The almost perfect storm of pressures including the impact of major changes to pensions, and increasing uncertainty over job security have dramatically changed the career paradigm.

Expectations, perspectives and perceptions need to be recalibrated. Understanding how to get the optimal **ROM** is the key. For example, many senior people are likely to be staying put rather than moving up or out as they come to terms with the reality of a lengthy recessionary environment, where new opportunities are harder to come by. In this context it is always worth exploring what might be available in one's current organisation. This may not necessarily be a promotion, but it may be a career strengthening opportunity such as:

- Involvement with a major project

- Secondment to a different department/function

- Deputising or taking the lead on a key piece of work

- Acting as a mentor for less experienced colleagues

- Development initiatives such as acquiring new skills or updating existing ones

A case in point is someone who declined their manager's offer of training to upgrade their accounting skills, who now finds themself passed over for promotion by outsiders with more relevant skills and current knowledge of accounting practices.

Whatever your experience of keeping yourself employable, in an uncertain economic environment, heightened concerns about the future "control" can become a major issue with counterproductive behaviours potentially causing low stability and high, often undirected energy. The majority of performance issues originate from concerns over roles, accountabilities and boundaries and people sometimes do themselves no favours in the way they seek clarity from their line manager about their current performance and future prospects. We all attach significance to inclusion and exclusion and may disengage, over time, in response to perceived career/development blockages. Self-awareness is a key skill to have at times such as this. Without it we may have no real sense of how we "land" on other people and the takeaway we leave with them.

Oliver Hibbert, an employee engagement specialist with Nexus Consulting, observes that: "Over your career, departments and job functions may change significantly; but you need to build recognition for your contribution and talent that will outlive job titles. The crucial skill for managing your career in this context is being able to sell your experience across the cultural boundaries of the company – you need to be able to think outside the box of your department and to engage with others across the organisation so that they understand your contribution and want to work with you. This means taking a hard look at the relationships you have in the organisation now and how they are working."

What are the elements of effective career management?

Firstly we need to be clear that "success" is a very personal issue. However, we should always be alert to the ways in which we can learn from others. The range of challenges – and opportunities – confronting us vary as do our individual responses. How might you deal with the following issues?

• Swingeing headcount reductions remove promotion opportunities locally with the only option to move to another location

• You have lost interest in your current career and at your age of fifty would really like to follow your instincts, but don't know if you can afford to

• The internal competition for roles is so intense you feel you will never move on

• Family circumstances have dramatically changed; you are the breadwinner and are concerned about your future employability

• You recently missed out on an internal promotion for which you feel you were ideally suited

• Although you have progressed since you left university and work for a large organisation, you don't seem to have accomplished too much on your own account but always as part of a team

• A relationship/marriage has ended and you feel the need to move on in every sense

- Elderly parents are becoming increasingly frail and you are contemplating a move to be closer to them

- Your business has been taken over and the portents don't look good for your long-term career prospects

Here are a range of responses from people who have needed to take action at differing stages in their lives to adjust their own career trajectory. They have experienced a range of outcomes and emotions as they have reviewed what they chose to do to enhance their own **ROM**:

- "How will this look or be perceived by others? How will it look on my CV? What message will this activity or qualification send to my manager or the company? Will there be career benefits down the track? Could this lead to more interesting work?"

- "I follow a spiritual practice that allows one to access a connection that goes beyond intuition. I followed the steer this was giving. However, I still remained grounded and undertook financial analysis to see how long I could withstand the lack of a steady income."

- "Very little (other than) could I do the job?; would it work for me and my family?; would it pay more, give me more influence and massage my ego?"

- "Honestly said, it was firstly my gut feeling and secondly my strong curiosity to get to know other companies and work in different cultures with other people. Knowing myself quite well, I thought I have still to learn and work in areas where I have some gaps."

- "I looked at potential employers' track records and financial performance; opportunities to continuously learn and develop and get the position I was seeking without compromise."

- "My own vision of the future."

- "Mostly self-interest in the sense that I tried to ensure that my choices would benefit me via the range of experiences, type of work or industry, promotion prospects, salary and benefits, job interest and doing things that I had not done before. I tried to get a balance between logical career decisions and personal aims and levels of happiness. I can't do a job long term if I am not happy in the work itself, even if it pays well."

Some of these descriptions will chime with you more than others; some readers may be muttering "I'd never do that" whilst others may be wondering "Why didn't I do that?" In part this depends on the place you go to under pressure: most of us default to a particular pattern of behaviour. It's "what we always do"! However, the utility of such an approach may be destructive rather than productive. A common default approach to career management is characterised by:

- A reactive rather than proactive approach – waiting for something to turn up

- Assuming their boss and/or employer "must know best" and are consequently cautious about actively seeking guidance and uncertain as to how to share their expectations and concerns without creating the "wrong" impression

- Adopting an unstructured approach to getting the next move, adopting an "up and out" strategy

- Going forth totally unprepared into a competitive labour market

The challenge is that when we are in the turbulent zone, we may be completely oblivious to the pattern we are falling into. Patterns matter! So identifying your own default is of some importance.

The importance of the choices to be made exemplifies this:

- "My decision (to become self-employed) increased the possibility of doing higher level jobs, albeit as projects, rather than long-term jobs. It gave lots of flexibility of working hours, the chance to work for a wide variety of organisations, and not having to get bogged down in the politics and culture of a business. It totally changed my working life – the best thing I ever did even though my overall pay and benefits package was probably less than I could have received by staying employed."

- "I chose to work in an industry which generally does well financially and where continuous learning and development is not constrained by funding."

- "There have been choices that have had an influence on many factors other than simply the role and my working environment. Where I live, the people that now form part of my circle of friends, the money I now earn and the lifestyle that I am able to lead have all been hugely affected."

- "It felt that there was really no choice. A deep inner conviction which manifested itself as a profound discomfort at physical and emotional levels made me realise that I had to get out of the line of business I was in."

- "For each choice, having influence, achieving fulfilment, earning more (although this became less important once I had attained a certain level of remuneration), being successful and lastly feeling important!"

Career management is a continuous process, sometimes misconstrued as a series of events. The risk of adopting an "event management" approach is that it can lead to disjointed and potentially unfulfilling outcomes. There are a series of steps in any career journey but these are interconnected rather than separated. Of particular importance is "mapping" and this book provides a range of ways to help you explore your current situation and leveraging your capability and capacity to make the best of your journey.

Mapping

Mapping is something we all do all of the time. It's how we make sense of our surroundings. If we feel lost we will generally take a closer look at where we are than if we are on familiar territory. Familiarity can breed complacency; consequently, wherever you think you are on your career journey, it is important to recalibrate your understanding of your strengths, deficits and true potential.

Wherever you are in your career journey, and whatever your situation, good mapping is good practice. It provides structured impetus for:

- The newly redundant

- Those unsettled by changes at work and considering what to do if made redundant

- People working for organisations currently offering the possibility of voluntary redundancy

- Individuals looking to return to work after a career break

- Those contacted by search firms and consequently prompted to question what they really want from their career and those who are finding it difficult to get interviews

- Anyone feeling that it is time to take stock of one's aspirations and the barriers to fulfilling them

A particular issue is to fully understand what exactly your situation is. This requires reflection before rushing to action. There are many sources of help which provide an invaluable insight into your motives and capability, all too often ignored in the rush to get back into the labour market or to move on. It is particularly important to avoid adopting a scattergun approach to sending out an inadequately prepared CV too soon to the wrong people for inappropriate jobs.

Planning

This is the step which provides the opportunity to verify assumptions, and get feedback from others on how you "show up", along with possible next steps. The essence is about creating a safe environment in which to test out hitherto unthinkable hypotheses on what you would like to happen next and the resources (knowledge, skills, and behaviours) required to do so.

The core elements of any plan are to begin by defining objectives and benefits. This book may well give you new perspectives on both objectives and perceived benefits. For example, you may currently have the overriding aim of "developing my career by moving on as quickly as possible". However, the following chapters explore what you need to do to put yourself in a position to identify opportunities within your current organisation as a first step, along with how to explore opportunities elsewhere.

Exploring

Different routes, different outcomes? This is the real-time follow-on from the backroom planning phase where ideas are ready to be tried out. Actively exploring different routes requires the sharing and testing of ideas and constructively and non-judgmentally processing others' perceptions and opinions. It must also draw on your plan and, to be successful, needs to be grounded on the work you will have done to seek, and reflect upon, feedback supported by a CV which is fit for purpose. Without this your career journey may take on the characteristics of a circular tour.

Demonstrating competence

Fundamental to demonstrating competence is developing a CV that shows your capability and capacity; ensuring that the "real" you is present at the interview; establishing goals and targets for job search/career shift; and regularly reviewing progress and potential derailers and hindrances. Without this nothing will happen! Getting the job is no pushover. That said, all too often the candidate does not live up to their billing. Failing to match the expectations created through the CV disappoints the potential employer and the subsequent rejection of a CV or after a poor interview frustrates the individual. A topical example is the first Obama-Romney debate where the President significantly underestimated his opponent. Understanding the perceptions and expectations of all the players in the process is critical, along with the message/impression you leave them with.

Arriving and delivering

You've got the job. Now the work starts!

Assimilation into a new role during the first 100 days requires both cultural understanding and a focus on delivering what's required. "Look, listen and learn" is important. For senior roles the capacity to hit the ground running and to deliver results in what may be a very different environment from the one anticipated, and described during the recruitment process, is critical.

Consolidating and reviewing

Career management does not end with successfully finding a new position, whether as CEO or graduate trainee. There will be a continuing need to choreograph your own career. The characteristics of effective career management remain important. What will you do to continue to maximise your **ROM** in the new role?

Choreography

For all of us, career management is best seen as the journey it is: sometimes uncomfortable, often great fun and periodically totally chaotic, no matter how much we have planned for each and every contingency. Many of us plan a career journey as if it were a day trip so care needs to be taken during the early stages!

Here is an example of the way in which a career can be choreographed:

What drove my career choices?

For my initial career choice this was really easy; I discovered a profession that has consistently been rated as one of the best jobs to have, pays very well and – most importantly – required something I was good at and enjoyed (maths). So I qualified (eventually) as an actuary.

Subsequently what I have looked for in my career boils down to two key factors. Firstly, to keep me and my family in the lifestyle we desired. That was fortunately quite easy, and if it had not been I think we would have adjusted lifestyle expectations to suit. Too many people seem to look down the wrong end of this particular telescope. The second factor, and the more important one in terms of overall satisfaction, was doing stuff I enjoyed. By that I mean work I found interesting and challenging, working with teams I found stimulating and fun, providing an overall sense of achievement.

I have though a low boredom threshold and a high intolerance of corporate politics. The combination meant that I would usually be looking for a fresh challenge every couple of years or so. That did not necessarily mean with a different company; I spent eleven years with a large reinsurer, during which time I had five quite different roles (marketing, client management, technical management, finance and new proposition development), mainly

---

working with a very professional and engaged group of people.

When the challenge has waned or the culture become something I did not want to be a part of it, has to be time to change. You just need to keep your eyes open for the opportunity. I don't particularly regard myself as a risk taker – and I still had a family to feed – but I was always prepared to back my abilities in a new environment or role rather than cling on to something I was not enjoying. So I moved firstly into financial services outsourcing, running an admin operation of some 500 people, then to developing a much smaller HR outsourcing business. Both areas were loosely connected to my insurance background, but both provided a range of new experiences.

My next role was more of a cultural challenge – to help lead the modernisation of a sleepy life office. My role as Chief Actuary meant getting them through a whole heap of technical challenges but the cultural aspects of the organisation were in many ways more fascinating. My final "proper" job was back in reassurance working with a number of previous colleagues in leading the turn-around of a business whose parent was badly hit by the 2007 credit crisis. They had some great new business ideas and we pioneered the development of longevity reassurance - both an interesting technical challenge and very satisfying to get the first few deals done under our belt. But once that became too much like business as usual, I decided that the only route left for me that provided the stimulation I still sought, without any politics, was to run my own consultancy business. I have done this happily for the last four years, although I am now winding it down to pursue a range of hobbies and interests that have nothing to do with insurance.

For most of my career choices I had no clear idea where they would take me, but in all of them I felt that they would provide a good challenge, some learning experiences and the opportunity to achieve something new. In all cases that is what happened.

In the words of the great Steve Winwood: "While you see a chance [just] take it."

The Takeaway

Most of us face a variety of challenges and barriers at some point in our careers. Taking a proactive role in the choreography of your career and developing your self-management capability will enable you to determine areas where you need to take action, where you require additional support and identify where you are already making progress.

The steps	Self-Management	Processes
Mapping	Balancing Focus & Desire	Feedback and the Performance Review
Planning		
Exploring	Insight	Outplacement, Executive Coaching and Mentoring
Demonstrating Competence		
Arriving & Delivering	Connecting	My Big Fat CV
Consolidating & Reviewing		

Chapter Three
Self-Management

"The world is moving so fast these days that the man who says it can't be done is generally interrupted by someone doing it."

Elbert Hubbard (1856-1915)

A sideways move rather than a promotion; a predatory takeover that imposes a new culture; redundancy, whether anticipated or not, all create a range of emotions ranging from anger to excitement. Looking back you may see such events as a personal watershed that led to unexpected and significant opportunities. At the time you may say, "I never saw that coming"; sometimes it is impossible to second guess corporate direction or strategy changes. However, if you are able to take a proactive approach to managing your career, some of these "surprises" may be avoided. A particular challenge is to avoid going to your default – the place you go when under pressure. In the context of career management this can lead to knee-jerk responses which may well provide short-term satisfaction leading to longer-term disappointment. Involving others in helping you see the situation from a different perspective can make a significant difference. Without this, actions taken too quickly with the aim of putting you "in control" may do the opposite:

- Closing in on yourself – "getting the wagons in a circle" and becoming withdrawn. As one Executive Director observed following the resignation of a highly valued colleague, "If they had spoken to their line manager earlier, rather than after finding a new role elsewhere, I'm sure we could have come up with something that worked for all of us. The cost of retaining an employee with potential is generally significantly less than going out into the market to recruit. Someone like this leaving also sends a negative signal to others about how we develop people and we also need to look at this."

- Renewing contact with a search firm that you came across in the past and hoping they can help. "Placing your faith in one search firm is a mug's game. You need to get yourself known across your desired market. All search firms are not the same."

- Rejecting outplacement: if you have been made redundant the offer of some assistance to get your next job would seem like something worth taking. However, a small number of people do reject this offer, generally as a means of maintaining some control over what they consider their right to choose what they do next. Not a good idea.

Without a plan and regular reviews of that plan, sporadic rather than concerted action is likely to result. A form of blunderbuss attack on the job market with an inadequate CV is unlikely to deliver dividends. Essentially self-management is the means by which you will increase the odds on improving your **ROM**. Without better understanding the connectivity of the career management process as a whole, the chances are you will become over-reliant on a particular approach or provider and potentially stuck at a step in your career journey from which you wish or need to move on.

Self-management is the bridge upon which your career journey depends. It provides the means to navigate the steps in your journey and the understanding to effectively draw on other resources and processes as you make your way forward. Effective self-management requires the capacity to choreograph a range of choices and activities. In large part this is all about the acquisition and utilisation of knowledge to enable you to make choices about how best to leverage your experience and commitment.

This "bridge" matters, since without an understanding of the characteristics discussed below you may place your destiny in the hands of a range of suppliers and consultants such as recruitment agencies, search firms or outplacement providers. All are useful, but you need to understand that what's important to you may not always be important to them. A case in point is a significant change in the recruitment market driven by a combination of technology and cost control. Once upon a time an agency may have held sole rights to recruitment whereas now you may find the same job being handled by a handful of agencies using job boards to elicit a response. They are working for a success fee; do not assume that your best interests guide their actions. Equally many search firms will cultivate relationships with high quality candidates and those they genuinely believe are going to be successful reasonably soon. There is nothing wrong with this, but as a candidate you need to recognise that you must maintain a constant oversight of your career journey and how best to keep them mindful of your profile.

There are three clusters of attributes which characterise effective self-management:

Balancing focus and desire

Focus combined with desire is powerful; one without the other leads to a distorted view of what's possible. Under duress – such as a job we are very unhappy with, the need to find a new job quickly to support our family, or a determination to show a former employer that they were wrong to make you redundant – we may default to a focus on activity. This results in countless failed applications and increasing frustration which lead to repeating the same – ineffective – behaviour. Alternatively you may have in mind an "ideal" job or a particular salary level that overrides taking a wider view of what is an acceptable rather than a "perfect" role.

Focus is required to understand the areas that are critical to success. Where are the most attractive opportunities? Do they match what I really want? Managing these two potentially competing attributes requires energy and awareness. A failure to do so shows up in many ways:

- Typos in your CV, usually caused by a desire to send this out as quickly as possible

- Becoming so enthusiastic about a role that you lose focus in responding to the interviewer's questions

- Your desire to move into a bigger line role persists, despite feedback to the contrary from a number of reliable sources suggesting a move to a similar role in a bigger organisation would be more appropriate

Desire is an invaluable companion to focus, generating resilience, energy and imagination. On the other hand, unchecked desire may lead to poor career choices. This may include joining an organisation without doing sufficient due diligence and subsequently discovering major balance sheet issues, or taking an "ideal" role in a smaller organisation which, it turns out, operates on a command and control basis – stifling your creativity and sapping your confidence.

Insight and outsight

All too frequently we are urged to understand the other person's point of view. Unfortunately, the prerequisite to doing this is overlooked, namely understanding and appreciating yourself. Developing awareness of personal strengths and deficits and understanding the importance of discovering how others see you is important. This awareness provides the basis for productive relationships and the impetus to better understand the environments you would like to work in. It also enhances your capacity to take a longer-term look at where your career may take you.

Additionally the capacity to take a look over the horizon and test out the validity of your career plans as economies, markets and labour needs change is also of great benefit. Self-management is not about doing everything by yourself and for yourself. Rather we all need to understand when support may be required. An acronym I came across years ago holds good here: STAN – Safe To Admit Need – is something we should all be aware of both personally and on behalf of others. Here are some examples of the variety of approaches adopted:

- "At the time I used a trusted mentor who was my manager. He recommended that I undertake the qualification. There is usually someone who will encourage you to take new steps. They will also see opportunities for you and encourage you to seek them out."

- "Spouse, friends, colleagues, or mostly previous colleagues."

- "My partner and, less so, colleagues and managers."

- "I discussed my ideas with my life partner but did not really access any other external help."

- "Family, friends and the counsel of colleagues who fall into the friends category. I try and go through every angle with a number of different parties, using those I trust as a sounding board but making the ultimate decision using my own instinct and views alone."

- "I asked my current and former bosses for their views about my plans to make a change. They were generally encouraging for me to go for the next step. But of course I also spoke with family and good friends."

- "I have never required professional advice on my intentions or choices and have always followed my own path, based upon information from my network of friends, as well as regular talks with previous HR advisors."

- "The mirror – didn't trust too many people to know what they were doing let alone tell me about what I was doing!"

- "Family plus my gut instinct; I didn't find many people with forward vision that could help me."

- "I didn't really seek advice; I just observed the market and made my own decisions. My entry to the care industry was initiated by my father as he recommended a social studies course, but from there I made my own decisions."

Reflecting on what might have been done differently elicited these responses:

- " I am very satisfied at this point in time yet very anxious about the imminent changes that lie ahead."

- "I have a fairly flexible nature and quite a high tolerance of corporate nonsense. My sense is that I ought to have done it more quickly and been more insistent in bringing my ex business partner to the table."

- "Pretty good really. I am never quite satisfied with anything I do but people seem to think I have done OK. Good pension, respect, impact on the communities I was seeking to help."

- "Overall I am satisfied. I have made mistakes, but that is part of the process. I certainly don't look back and regret what I have done; I perhaps regret that I didn't have more confidence in myself when I was younger and less experienced."

- "Mixed. I am paid very well and, yes, some of the work is interesting and different. I enjoy working with interesting people, usually in a team. Unfortunately this hasn't eventuated. I see many opportunities being lost because of poor and unstrategic management."

- "Given my background with no university degree I am very satisfied to have achieved quite a lot."

- "Very satisfied, I enjoy work every day and feel well appreciated."

- "I can really accomplish just about anything I set my mind to if I am willing to commit the resources to achieving it; self-cultivation (continued growth) of body, mind and spirit is imperative to accomplish goals and stay sane."

- "Bearing in mind the economic climate these were the right decisions – but it's still a work in progress."

- "Fairly satisfied although never really feel like I have achieved enough and have started looking elsewhere for opportunities. Ideally I would like to study more, but trying to balance family and work life is hard enough, so trying to put study in there as well would be impossible."

As you can see there is variety here. One size does not fit all circumstances. But all the respondents did, to varying degrees, involve others in the process of determining what to do next. This happened at various stages and with a mix of people, some from work others from their family. An interesting observation on whether anything could have been done differently elicited this response: "Not really. I would see it that anything which I am not entirely happy with is more down to me as a person rather than anything I could have done differently; and how much am I going to be able to change? The most important thing I can learn from now is to be happy with what I have achieved and trust the process will bring me where I need to be."

Connecting

"Connected" individuals recognise the importance of networking. Networking is one of the words of the 21st century, yet for many a goal rather than a reality. The reality is frequently a passive list of contacts on one of the many professional or social networks. The sheer number, rather than the quality of relationships you have with your network, is also often over-rated. In reality many of us profess to be networking when in reality our approach is "notworking". Be aware that:

- You ignore networking at your peril

- Networking will not of itself get you a new job but it may set off a chain of events that lead you to a point at which you may be offered a new job

- You have many more potential network contacts than you realise. Subsequent chapters explore a range of sources for identifying them

This comment exemplifies the potential benefits: "As yet less than three weeks after the event there is no new job yet I am left with a sense of freedom and optimism. I am networking with a selected group of contacts and friends from the insurance market. I made an announcement via Facebook and LinkedIn that I had quit my job and open to sensible discussions, which quickly produced a response."

The description below is from someone yet to graduate and illustrates how their own "sandwich" degree course has required them to gain and utilise skills to seek internships. The acquisition of networking skills at this point in one's career will bear dividends over the longer term as this individual recognises: "I feel I have learnt more about the professional working world this year than I have over the first two years at university and I know these experiences will help me in preparation for my final year and after I graduate."

"I've done five internships so far and they've all been quite different in the process of getting them, and I had to apply for lots without even hearing a word back from anyone a lot of the time. It seems that once you get the first internship it is easier to find another as contacts will develop and people I've interned for always seem happy to point me in a useful direction for finding more work.

The first internship I did was for Company A which was actually a contact made through my university and was a competition really, out of the 40 of us doing the year out, six of our portfolios were selected by our tutors on our assessment day – mine being one of them. One of the creative directors came to interview us and look through our work and three of us won a two-week internship and £800 overall. So that was a bit of luck and pretty simple to get really as I didn't have to do any of the legwork!

After sending lots of e-mails to different design studios that I had found out about and researched – some I found out about through my tutor, others I had discovered by researching on blogs, magazines and books – basically any work that I liked I would find out what studio designed it and research them and would try and get in contact. Although e-mailing 'info@designstudio.com' rarely gets a reply and it seems you need an exact point of contact to get in touch with if you want a response – it's definitely more about who you know than what you know.

I'm lucky as my Professional Studies Tutor has loads of contacts, and studios often get in touch with her to ask if she has any students that are looking for internships, so she often sends out e-mails to all of us on the year out to let us know. Two of my internships have been gained this way. If you are quick to respond and arrange an interview with them ASAP then you can beat the other 39 students to it – I think a lot of the studios don't have time to spend choosing between students so they will go with whoever is the first one to come along who seems alright!

The other two were studios that I had approached myself. Like with my other applications to the two studios I knew were looking for an intern, I e-mailed in to the studio with a covering letter, telling a bit about myself and the year out I'm doing and what I like about their studio and the work they do. I also attached a PDF to the e-mail with a selection of my work that I have done and a CV. They then offered me an interview and portfolio review where I bring in my work and talk them through it and we discuss the role of an intern at their studio and my interests etc.

All in all it's quite a long process so once someone agrees to let you come in and work for free (although I have always had some expenses paid for – some have been quite generous, i.e. £150/week where others have been more stingy and would only pay for my Oyster zones 1-2 so long as I kept my receipts) then I jump at the chance! It's so competitive, and I'm competing against designers who have already graduated for these roles as it seems everyone has to work for free for a while these days before anyone is willing to take you on full time – even if you have a degree. So you can't afford to be fussy and the experiences are so valuable to have. I feel I have learnt more about the professional working world this year than I have over the first two years at university and I know these experiences will help me in preparation for my final year and after I graduate."

Although there are many organisations which continue to advertise roles, it is networking that can alert you to opportunities that may never be advertised and dramatically increase your access to them through proactive contact with recruiters and search firms. A very simple measure of your current connectivity is how you rate your activity level in the following potential sources of jobs:

- Regularly review press advertising:
  - National
  - Local
  - Trade press
- Regularly review internet networks:
  - Professional including job boards
  - Social
- Academic links:
  - Careers service
  - Alumni networks
- Current, former and potential employers
  - Regularly review websites
  - Alumni networks
- Regular contact with search firms
- Regular contact with recruitment agencies

Be honest with yourself in responding to this. At this stage a passive approach is better than directing a poor CV reflecting uncertain career goals.

The structure of this book is designed to provide a template for action rather than demand slavish adherence, so make a note when you see something that may be of potential use to you and test out how useful it is.

Also be aware that many of us when faced with a new, apparently insurmountable challenge will revert to our default of doing what we've always done. These patterns can produce unproductive behaviours that impede our progress. The paradox is that when we are doing this and could really use some help to find another way, we are at our most resistant to feedback. Challenges come in many forms with losing one's job or being passed over for promotion two of the more obvious ones. The boredom induced by a job you really don't enjoy is an equally potent trigger for default behaviours.

The examples below from two individuals in their early career journey provide more reinforcement for the need to seek advice, but also to think carefully about the criteria against which to assess the choices available. There are going to be occasions when you cannot get what you want, so the capacity to take a longer-term perspective and be prepared to make trade-offs in the meantime without compromising your long-term goals is important.

Example one

A. WHAT HAVE BEEN YOUR MOST IMPORTANT CAREER CHOICES?
My most important career choices to date include choosing to study a sandwich degree in which a year of my studies was spent working full time in a role that I was interested in pursuing after completing my degree.

After university, I opted to join a small and fast-growing company rather than applying for graduate schemes in larger companies.

Once I qualified as a Chartered Accountant, I chose to move to a bigger, co-ownership company.

B. WHAT MADE THE CHOICE(S) SO IMPORTANT?

Opting to complete a placement year enabled me to see how the theory of what I was studying was applied in practice. The year also helped me to confirm my decision to pursue a career in Finance. I also found that when applying for roles as a graduate, my year in industry was vital in securing permanent employment quickly.

When choosing to work for a smaller company, I felt doing so would allow me to gain more exposure to many different aspects of the company. This turned out to be very rewarding as I worked closely with higher management which enabled me to work with a higher level of responsibility than I would have in a larger company. I produced a lot of information for the Board on a regular basis. I was also able to support the tender process when the company was refinanced. This was great exposure and helped me tremendously when studying for my accountancy qualification.

C. WHAT CRITERIA DID YOU USE TO MAKE YOUR CHOICE(S)?

The criteria I used to make my choices were those that would enable me to develop myself and my skills the most. I also made these choices based on whether they would challenge me sufficiently and how they would help me to progress in my career. I also felt it was important to pursue roles which excited and interested me.

D. FROM WHOM DID YOU SEEK ADVICE ON YOUR INTENTIONS?

I sought advice from my parents as well as career advisers at both school and university. I also found speaking with colleagues and friends provided me with valuable insight and a broad range of perspectives.

E. DESCRIBE THE OUTCOME(S) (E.G. NEW JOB/NEW EMPLOYER/CHANGE OF CAREER DIRECTION)

The above decisions have enabled me to gain employment with a great company with great rewards. My company both invests in and develops its employees which is very important to me. I have gained a lot of experience and learnt a lot of new skills as well as developing my existing skills further. This has helped me to progress quickly within my current company.

F. HOW SATISFIED ARE YOU WITH THE OUTCOME(S)?

Very satisfied, I thoroughly enjoy my current role and feel there are plenty of development opportunities for me at my current employer and beyond should I wish to progress elsewhere. I also feel my career as a Finance Analyst would enable me to move into different areas of the company should I wish to. The skills I have gained are highly transferable to other areas of the business.

G. LOOKING BACK, DO YOU FEEL THERE IS ANYTHING YOU COULD HAVE DONE DIFFERENTLY; WHAT HAS BEEN YOUR MOST SIGNIFICANT LEARNING FROM THE EXPERIENCE?

I don't feel there is anything I could have done differently to date as I have found all my roles to be very rewarding in different ways. My most significant learning is that it's important to challenge yourself and pursue roles which interest you. Without these factors it can be difficult to find the drive to push yourself to the best of your ability.

Example two

A. WHAT HAVE BEEN YOUR MOST IMPORTANT CAREER CHOICES?

- Whether to seek employment at the end of my (archaeology) degree or whether to complete a master's degree.

- When to start a family.

B. WHAT MADE THE CHOICE(S) SO IMPORTANT?

- By not completing a master's degree I shut off most heritage sector jobs on the career paths.

- I knew that I did not want to immediately return to full-time work after the birth of my son so I had to decide when in my career it would be appropriate to take a break.

C. WHAT CRITERIA DID YOU USE TO MAKE YOUR CHOICE(S)?

- Financial. I could not self-fund an MSc and lacked the self-confidence to push to try to obtain funding. I was engaged and my husband wanted to start his own business so we agreed the best time to do it was when neither of us had any-thing to lose, however this meant that one of us needed to find employment in something stable. Heritage jobs that you can do with just an undergraduate degree are poorly paid and often mean moving around a lot which was not some-thing I was prepared to do at that point in my life.

- When I felt that I had reached a point in my career where I had sufficient experience and a solid skills base, which would mean I was employable even with a break from full-time teaching. When my husband's career was at a point that we could afford for me not to have a full-time income.

D. FROM WHOM DID YOU SEEK ADVICE ON YOUR INTENTIONS?

- Husband, friends on my degree course

- Husband, close colleagues

E. DESCRIBE THE OUTCOME(S) (E.G. NEW JOB/NEW EMPLOYER/CHANGE OF CAREER DIRECTION)

- I feel I have closed the door on working in the heritage sector and will never use my first class BSc in Archaeology. Going into secondary science teaching gave me financial security but was a huge change of career direction from where I thought I would go.

- By taking an extended maternity break I have had the opportunity to try lots of teaching-related activities such as private tutoring, GCSE marking and primary supply teaching, all of which have greatly furthered my skills base.

F. HOW SATISFIED ARE YOU WITH THE OUTCOME(S)?

- Bit sad but ended up working in a much more employable sector which has hopefully enabled me to have a more family-friendly career.

- Glad that I had the chance to work as head of department before I took a break and pleased that I have been able to spend time with my son whilst still having the skills to do a range of jobs to fit around what I want to do.

G. LOOKING BACK DO YOU FEEL THERE IS ANYTHING YOU COULD HAVE DONE DIFFERENTLY; AND WHAT HAS BEEN YOUR MOST SIGNIFICANT LEARNING FROM THE EXPERIENCE?

- I wish I had taken the risk and tried applying for MSc places and funding. I have learnt that I am fortunate and that my best is often **the** best and I need to have more confidence in myself.

- Wouldn't have done anything differently. Was worried that having only worked in one school would be a disadvantage but having sought work recently it has not been a problem and the range and level of skills on my CV has been well regarded.

At this point it would be useful to contemplate – and retain – your own response to these questions:

- What have been your most important career choices?

- What made the choice(s) so important?

- What criteria did you use to make your choice(s)?

- From whom did you seek advice on your intentions?

- Describe the outcome(s) (e.g. new job/new employer/change of career direction)

- How satisfied are you with the outcome(s)?

- Looking back do you feel there is anything you could have done differently; what has been your most significant learning from the experience?

What is this telling you about your own approach to:

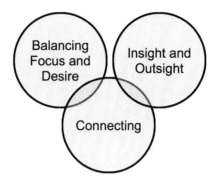

And the extent to which you are working on all three? With this in mind, this is a good moment for reflection. A number of people who were kind enough to read the draft text commented that a variety of themes rang true for them and their needs, but they then felt overwhelmed at the prospect of making sense of what might be required. So please don't panic; plan!

An effective plan requires reflection and adaptation as well as action. Many readers will be doing a considerable amount already; however, an additional, albeit slight, shift in direction may make a considerable difference to your understanding and the outcome. To that end here is an opportunity to take stock of your current approach and identify areas where there may be an opportunity to gain fresh insight by identifying your current level of understanding of the themes and actions addressed in this book. The matrix below asks you to rate both your current level of understanding and your effectiveness. For example you may be very familiar with the importance of networking but not enjoy making contact; so you might rate this as 9/10 for understanding, but only 2/10 for accomplishment. Or you may consider yourself to have a strong CV but feel that the "real" you is not wholly present during an interview, which would suggest low scores for accomplishment in "demonstrating competence" and "feedback".

Please rate each factor on a regular basis to track your progress, assessing your understanding of what is required, and your sense of accomplishment in terms of having successfully delivered and/or completed what is necessary.

		Current level of understanding 0=low/10=high	Current level of effectiveness 0=low/10=high
STEPS			
Mapping	How well do I understand my current situation?		
Planning	What next – the potential options and resources required		
Exploring	How aware am I of the opportunities available to me? Testing out opportunities		
Demonstrating competence	Does my CV and interview technique currently support my strengths, ambitions and the needs of potential employers?		
Arriving and delivering	What needs to be done to make a difference early in a new role		
Consolidating and reviewing	How will I enhance my reputation in the new organisation and maintain a longer-term focus?		
SELF-MANAGEMENT			
Balancing focus and desire	Ensuring a balanced approach to targeting the right jobs for the right reasons		
Insight	How self-aware am I? How well do I understand how others perceive me? What opportunities are available to me?		
Connecting	Spotting the opportunities that match my goals at the right time. How good a networker am I?		

PROCESSES			
Feedback and the Performance Review	Recent feedback from peers and others? How well do I understand my organisation's Performance Review Process?		
Outplacement, executive coaching and mentoring	How well do I understand these processes and the benefits they might provide?		
My Big Fat CV	Do I have a "master" CV that supports my understanding of my career drivers and ambitions and demonstrates my competence?		

The Takeaway

Successful career management requires a range of actions and insights. It's all too easy to become overwhelmed and "do what I always do". Taking stock of where you are now is an important step toward adopting a more proactive approach to getting what you want from your career.

Chapter Four
Feedback and the Performance Review

"A wonderful gift may not be wrapped as you expect."

Jonathan Lockwood Huie

Chapters Four, Five and Six explore a number of important processes which, when deployed in the context of self-management, will support your career journey. Depending on your circumstances, some of them may be provided by your current employer as part of your on-going development or as part of a severance package. Some have no "cost" but will require time and the support of others, along with your own desire to make progress.

This chapter looks at how to proactively seek and subsequently reflect upon feedback. It also exemplifies the importance of ensuring you understand how you are perceived at work and the role of the performance management in this process. Without proactively seeking feedback you put yourself at a disadvantage.

Feedback

365 degree feedback may be a label you will wish to attach to this, since feedback from various sources based on various situations is invaluable, not just the 360 degree feedback you may

have experienced at work. So talk to people who know you well, not just work colleagues. Whilst receiving feedback may sometimes be a challenge, giving it can be even more problematic. A colleague once remarked that after giving what she personally felt was a poor presentation, for her boss to tell her "it was a great job" indicated that it was much worse than she thought!

It may be that the feedback you receive through your organisation's performance review is very useful; however it is still worth calibrating this feedback by utilising the suggestions below.

My own experience of receiving feedback has sometimes been unsettling; particularly having to nominate a range of people from whom an external consultant would elicit responses and observations. It was the consultant who delivered the feedback, and whilst initially the thought of a third party acquiring and delivering the feedback may appear attractive, it does have a number of quite significant drawbacks:

- The very act of using an intermediary disempowers both giver and receiver. In multinational organisations this may be the only route available; however, the defect still remains.

- A third party is unable to respond in sufficient detail to the desire of the receiver to know "what makes you say that; tell me more; give me some more examples."

- The third party route may inadvertently provide a very convenient let out for all of us in providing a means to avoid giving and receiving feedback directly, face to face. The consequence is that the organisation and its people lose a great opportunity to bring authenticity to workplace dialogue.

To overcome the logistical challenges in organisations with a dispersed workforce and more generally to reduce costs, an alternative has emerged in the form of on-line feedback processes. Although a number of commentators have suggested that the on-line approach improves the quality of dialogue by giving both parties the time to make considered responses, a particular challenge with this approach is the lack of direct contact between provider and recipient. This can lead to an absence of accountability for the feedback provided and a sense of disempowerment on the part of the receiver. An additional – and very real – issue is that of "feedback fatigue" when the focus is on responding to a large number of requests as a precursor to the annual performance review season. Quantity rather than quality may become paramount. The paradox is that feedback without accountability and ownership is perpetuating decision-making behind closed doors and preventing individuals having the opportunity to better understand the way in which they are perceived by others. This actually is a very big deal since honest feedback, sensitively delivered, can make a massive difference to all our careers. As discussed earlier, feedback needs to be integrated into daily working life as an ongoing process – not an annual event.

Taking care to ensure that you personally seek feedback from others is important. If you are out of work it is a means of getting a sense of what your strengths are along with areas of potential or possible weakness and getting some pointers on your future direction. If you are unhappy in your current role it is a way of checking out how your future employability in the organisation is perceived by those in a position to help you. And if you feel you are "doing fine" it is a way of benchmarking how others perceive your contribution and avoiding future surprises. The challenge is who do you ask, how do you ask, and what should you ask? The label of 365 degree feedback is to remind you that friends, family, former colleagues and customers not now directly connected to your workplace can give you a view from differing perspectives rather than one which is solely work centred. Indeed those close to you may have detected unease on your part with a job or project some time before you were consciously aware of this. These are the people that may see a shift in your usual pattern of behaviour and their insight is valuable.

Following some simple rules will help the process operate constructively.

The **first** and foremost rule is to remember that to get the best **ROM** it is important to understand how others see you.

For many, the natural reaction is to feel comfortable about discussing things with your best colleague, less so with the "difficult" customer. Although you may feel "comfortable" with someone, this does not guarantee accurate feedback. People who work together for a long time develop "workarounds" to accommodate each other. Someone you feel is a "difficult" customer may have a high regard for your level of expertise and professionalism. But until you seek feedback your perception will remain just that.

To move forward you need to get yourself used to the process of seeking feedback, comfortable at handling the process of receiving feedback and then making sense of it. You may well have people in mind that can help you, so identify a short list of up to five people you believe would be prepared to assist. This could include colleagues, team mates or family members.

Do not be seduced or disappointed by your first experience; you need to focus on patterns that emerge as you explore how others see you. You may be markedly more enthusiastic when refereeing your son's football matches than at work, or you may be told you "live for your work". It is well worth reflecting on all these comments.

Consequently the **second** rule is to be clear about the purpose and method of seeking feedback. If you want your ego massaging you are unlikely to want to do this. For those with the desire to understand themselves better this can be achieved by outlining your situation and explaining how feedback would be of use to you:

- As you know, I was recently made redundant and I'm looking at the next step in my career. I would be grateful if you could give me some feedback to help me as I look at my options.

- I'm asking a number of people to help me; people who have seen me in the work environment and/or socially.

- It's important to me to get accurate feedback; I know people are generally sympathetic about redundancy, which I appreciate. But I also need to explore my strengths and areas where I could potentially do better so your help would be appreciated. It would be really useful if you can recall specific examples as well as your general observations on my approach to work.

- I would welcome some feedback on my performance and how you see my career progressing. What would be really useful are examples of work I've done and your thoughts on whether I could have done things differently. It will be helpful if you are able to describe the outcome you feel I achieved and the extent to which this was successful.

- I would like to do this face to face. To help you, I have a list of questions and would be happy to send this to you in advance.

Here are examples of questions which will elicit constructive feedback. The first asks about competence. If you are lacking the competence to do something, there may be a number of reasons, including inadequate support or training; of itself this does not make you a failure. It is also important to be aware that having the knowledge and the skill may not lead to one actually delivering or executing a task in the right way. The "what" and the "how" of your performance both matter; feedback can alert you to possible mismatches as well as alerting you to your hidden strengths or competencies you personally underrate:

- I'm keen to get your views on my competence when we worked together in terms of knowledge, skills and behaviours

- Describe my strengths as a supplier/colleague/team member

- What do I do well; what could I do differently?

- Describe my development needs

- If you had the power to get me to change just one aspect of my approach to work, what would it be?

- What would you like more of from me as a supplier/colleague/team member?

- What would you like less of from me?

- If you had one gift which would modify my behaviour, what would that be?

- If at this moment you had the opportunity to send me a message that would help me to focus on your comments, what would that be?

- Based on what you know of me, what are your thoughts on my next step?

- Is there anything else you feel would be useful for me to know?

The work you will do on My Big Fat CV (later in this book) may raise questions or themes you would also like to explore in some of these feedback sessions, so feel free to include them. There are no "right" answers to these questions. They are aimed at helping you start the process of better understanding your career motivations and beginning to interrogate yourself on cause and effect. This is important because it is positioning you as your career manager rather than a third party where others drive your career management.

The **third** rule is to be open to your feelings. Do not put yourself into neutral gear, going through the process of receiving feedback but inwardly switching off or explaining to oneself why something is irrelevant or not part of the whole picture. So accept that being open to the process is a learning experience that will potentially give you new insights.

The **fourth** rule is to listen and make notes if you wish. Interrupting to say "you've got that out of context" is not helpful at this stage. Asking for more information is perfectly acceptable after your feedbacker has completed each segment:

- Tell me more about that.

- What exactly did you observe?

- Can you give me a few examples?

- What other choices might I have taken?

- Avoid the use of the word "but" to rebut comments. You need to reboot, not rebut.

It can also be useful to ask your feedbacker to apply a numerical rating to some of their observations. So, if you are given feedback about a sales call and get the feedback that "I would have done that rather differently and got to the close a little quicker", you might ask: "If you had to rate that what would you score it, with one being poor and ten being excellent?" This can help you get a sense of how this particular individual ranks you against others rather than potentially misreading some feedback as an absolute score.

The **fifth** rule is to approach each feedback session as a gift, not as a punishment.

It would be naive to pretend the logistics of setting up each session are always straightforward. Finding a time and place may be difficult, although use a telephone discussion if all else fails.

After each session, use the template below to record your thoughts and feelings. Revisit your notes a few days later having given yourself a day to reflect on what was said and what you heard.

How do I feel about this session?	
Did I listen enough?	
What surprised me?	
What pleased me?	
What displeased me?	
Do I need to add/delete any questions?	

What actions do I need to take as a result of this feedback?	
Have I thanked my feedbacker and asked for their thoughts on others who might be able to help me?	

In reviewing the feedback you have received, please remember that the purpose of seeking feedback is not to force you into a new or different pattern of behaviour that does not reflect the real you. Imitating others is not a good idea, whereas understanding yourself better is a great gift. To reiterate a point made earlier, you will need to seek a range of feedback from a variety of people. From this, patterns are likely to emerge; talk to those you trust to test out the accuracy of your understanding of these patterns.

The performance review

For most of us, we hope to get a sense of how we are doing at work in delivering – or exceeding – the required level of performance and fulfilling our potential. Our boss plays a key role in this. Depending on the circumstances, this can range from daily to once a year. Once a year places a huge amount of importance upon the performance review process and is of course a totally inadequate means of managing someone. The "annual" performance review is not a justification or proxy for once-a-year feedback! However, despite the money invested in "improving" the performance management process – often by making it far too complex – you will frequently need to take the initiative in seeking feedback.

The diagram below is a generic look at the components of a performance review. To help the process help you, it's worth taking the time to familiarise yourself with how the process works in your own organisation. In theory, in any organisation the key driver is the business plan from which objectives will be set and cascaded to operating units and in turn to teams and individuals. For most of us a key issue is "line of sight" – what is the consequence of fulfilling all my objectives? The perceived value of the "reward" for so doing will vary. For some, recognition and career progression may be more significant in the longer term than a large one-off bonus. For others, the reward package will be a key aspect.

The impact of performance management processes from an organisational perspective is reviewed in Chapter Eleven. For the individual, having a good understanding of the competence framework which is used to support many systems is useful. This will give you a better feel for the qualities required to be effective and successful. Put simply these frameworks describe the knowledge, skills and behaviours required. Some are remarkably complex and are not fit for purpose; others add a great deal of value to an employee's awareness of what is required to do their job satisfactorily and provide a means to have a dialogue with your employer on what you will need to be able to do – or be perceived to be able to do – to get to the next level in the organisation. Although the "Performance" box shows "actual achievement and observed competence" as key ingredients, this is not always the case. As the examples below illustrate, impressions are formed and opinions expressed that may be very subjective.

Equally the "good" news delivered at the annual appraisal may not be that reliable; an individual told they are "the natural successor" to their boss may be in for a disappointment when someone else gets the job. Placing your reliance on one set of feedback once a year is not a great idea. Neither is failing to take the time to understand how your organisation's talent and career development processes operate and identifying what might be appropriate to your own needs. Waiting to be included is very polite but not a good tactic.

PERFORMANCE & TALENT MANAGEMENT

| Talent Supply | ⇨ | Business Plan | ⇦ | Demand for Talent |

Unit objectives

| **Competencies**
• Skills
• Know how
• Behaviour | Individual Objectives | **Performance**
• Achievement
• Observed competence |

| **Training & Development**
• Skills training
• Management training
• Development programmes | Feedback
Mentoring
Coaching | **Reward**
• Pay systems
• Line of sight
• Recognition
• Career progression |

When feedback comes too late

At this point, by way of a wake-up call, the list below shows a range of reasons for dismissal; some fair, some clearly unfair. These are real examples based on data from a number of lawyers and broadly fall into two principal clusters:

Reputational and/or circumstantial:

- There is "evidence" that they have been having some form of relationship with a member of staff or family of the boss

- They just don't look the part

- They have the reputation of a bully outside work

- They have inappropriate outside interests

Commitment and/or capacity related:

- They don't work hard enough

- They are making too many mistakes

- Personal hygiene issues

- They have a chip on their shoulder and haven't delivered for the last ten years

- They haven't moved along with the business and changed with the times

- They seem to take an inordinate amount of sick leave

- They are "difficult" and difficult to manage

- Lazy

- Too talkative, always socialising at work

- We've got to get the headcount down

- Too much time off

- Engaged, skilled and effective, but on their terms with their own goals – don't appear to share our vision for the business

- Raised a grievance against the boss

- They want to work part time

- Spends a lot of time dealing with trade union activities

- It's their time – no obvious reason other than the boss says they need to change but cannot put their finger on what precisely needs to shift

- They want to work/are working part time which does not fit the efficiency needs of the business

Some of these are discriminatory and unfair reasons for selection for dismissal and you may be shocked that this could happen. No doubt many of these assessments would have little substance if investigated further; they may well be based on the reputation an individual has acquired or is perceived to have. A number of the people involved may have great potential and these descriptions say more about poor management than individual failings. That said, there are innumerable examples of employees who only discovered the misperceptions their employers had of them far too late. There are also individuals who are continually surprised that their behaviour has not been challenged.

Members of the "awkward squad" are often bright people with a job that does not provide an adequate degree of stretch or interest. Many of us have seen someone cast aside by one organisation move on to perform exceptionally well in another. The question you may be asking yourself is, "Why wasn't something said or done about these issues?" Despite the considerable sums spent on performance management processes, there is much evidence that for various reasons the desire and capacity of those responsible for giving feedback is lacking. We touched on the issue of not wishing to give "bad" news earlier. Yet losing your job after ten years of apparently poor performance or unacceptable behaviour which has never been discussed with you is no doubt even worse news. A frequent difficulty is the absence of a common language to describe performance and inconsistent approaches to defining superior and inadequate performance. Changing the process year after year doesn't help either since it may weaken the confidence of line managers in the system, confuse employees and deliver inconsistent feedback.

As the preceding diagram shows, individual objectives are right at the heart of this process. Irrespective of your line manager's attitude to updating them to reflect changes in responsibility, they really should matter to you! A surprising number of managers move into a new role without a clear understanding of what they are actually expected to do and how they are expected to operate. Proactively taking the lead and developing your own job description for discussion with your boss will always draw out differences of emphasis and understanding. This is not a prescription for conflict; it is actually the best way to focus on agreement using constructive dialogue to explore differences and gaps.

Sadly this approach does not always work and however much a manager wants their people to take personal ownership of their development and performance, both parties must be willing participants. A support team member in a professional services practice was perceived by their boss to be weak on some key aspects of their personal organisation and that of managing the logistics of meetings on behalf of other team colleagues. The manager consequently organised a monthly catch up with the individual to discuss their collective thoughts on how the previous month had gone. These were described as coaching meetings rather than performance management. Recently the employee asked for the meetings to be stopped since they were stressful. When asked how they would both be able to review issues and needs on an on-going basis if these meetings were not to take place, the response was, "I don't know – that's your concern, you are the manager."

In reality, performance management and career reviews can be seen as a chore rather than a necessity by line managers. Reviews are completed to meet deadlines rather than to provide substance for an adult-to-adult conversation on possibility and reality. This is not to criticise line managers; they play a pivotal role which, despite years of delayering, remains key to engaging an organisation's people. Notwithstanding these comments, the performance review does present you with an opportunity to initiate a discussion on your prospects. The corporate implications of this are discussed in Chapter Eleven; for the moment consider your own position and your feelings about asking questions such as:

- "What do I need to be doing more of to get myself in position to be considered for a new role?"

- "Could we have a separate discussion on how I see my career evolving? I really enjoy my current job and would appreciate your guidance in taking a longer-term view."

The questions are broadly similar, but how you frame the question and how it lands on your boss really matter. The first variation may be heard as "I really want to move out of my role here"; not necessarily what you meant and probably not what your boss wants to hear. The second is a request – not a challenge – and positioned outside the immediate discussion, which also pays your boss the compliment of seeking advice from someone you trust.

In the context of the **ROM**, your performance review is an opportunity to seek ideas and feedback. Many individuals at all levels show surprising hesitation in doing this. The most commons reasons are:

- My boss is very busy/never has time

- I did arrange a meeting but we were both too busy to attend

- We don't have a great relationship

- A client meeting got in the way

- A project is under great pressure; there is simply no time

Are these plausible reasons? Up to a point, but if you don't ask you don't get. Underpinning a reticence to take this step is the frequently made assumption that the boss should be taking the initiative. Indeed the following are often cited as the characteristics of a "good" boss:

- Tells me what's going on

- Respects me as a person and as a professional

- Helps me to develop my skills and career and as a person

- Sets clear, achievable and challenging objectives

- Regularly gives me feedback

- Understands what motivates me

- Behaves with integrity

- Is fair

Your own line manager may share all or some of these characteristics. Maybe not; the characteristics of the effective self-manager show up in those people who take the initiative to get some time with their boss. This is, incidentally, a useful means of differentiating yourself. It may well take a degree of stamina to persist when meetings frequently get rescheduled and the choice as to whether to continue is ultimately yours. And if the relationship with the boss isn't great, that should not dissuade you from having this discussion. You might be surprised by the outcome. There is a saying that people don't leave organisations, they leave managers. A poor relationship with your current manager should not preclude a move within the organisation, but to make the right move for the right reasons will require you to work on reviewing what you really want and getting feedback on how others actually see you. The tyranny of the time lapse is something regular one-to-one discussions with your boss can offset. Feedback must be timely.

It is also important to recognise that the majority of organisations are grappling with major issues ranging from cost control, changes in consumer behaviour, regulatory frameworks and volatility in raw material costs. This is not an easy time to be a line manager. As organisations become complex and projects increasingly dominate the working day, job boundaries and role clarity are less certain which, of itself, potentially increases workplace conflict and tension. It is not only organisations that are shedding labour that experience this; your boss may be under as much pressure as yourself.

Timing makes a difference; asking for a discussion in the midst of the business planning season or as year-end accounts are being prepared is not likely to be greeted with too much enthusiasm. However, the ways in which people may get a lucky break can be positively impacted if you are able to get your perspective across before business planning or performance reviews enter their formal phase.

It's also important to remember that increasing your **ROM** is not just about promotion. Recognition and the opening of routes which lead in the right direction can take a variety of forms. If instant gratification is your aim, beware of what you wish for. Rather than an instant promotion, the following may provide the means by which you will progress in the longer term and additionally enhance your employability in the wider market:

- Training

- Retraining

- Mentoring

- Secondment

- Executive coaching

That said, it would be unrealistic to assume there will always be a positive outcome. You may have a supervisor who is a believer in "do nothing and hope for the best" or leaving it up to the individual to make their own case. In either situation, ask for a follow-up discussion with your boss's boss.

A real success may be no outcome other than creating a more effective working relationship by taking the initiative; a step which will have longer-term benefit than being sent on a training course of little relevance to your needs!

If not your line boss, would it be productive to speak to your HR colleagues? I always reckoned that those who would be successful in any business took the time to periodically remind me that they were interested in how their careers would progress. This did not result in preferential treatment but their networking did mean they were on my radar and were not forgotten when potential new roles were discussed.

The Takeaway

Seeking – and using – feedback can be a challenging process to initiate but the benefit is considerable.

Chapter Five
Outplacement, Executive Coaching and Mentoring

"It's never too late to be what you might have been."

George Eliot

This chapter reviews the role of outplacement, executive coaching and mentoring; outlining what they are and the benefits they may provide, along with the questions to ask as you assess their relevance to your own situation.

Outplacement

In the "old" world, outplacement provided support for individuals who lost their job. There are many providers who continue to offer support, and this is described below. In the context of **ROM** it is arguable that by the time you receive outplacement it may be a year too late.

The framework upon which this book is based enables a number of actions to be taken to continually scan the current and future horizon as a proactive career manager. It would be foolish to assume that the support outplacement provides is only relevant if you are out of a job. Proactively managing your career in your current organisation is equally important. As discussed in Chapter Four, understanding your own organisation's performance review is a good place to start.

Rather than waiting for the knock on the door and the offer of outplacement, proactive self-managers will be focusing on their own "inplacement" – working out what they really want and the steps they need to take to fulfil their goals.

My first project upon joining a large consulting firm was to assist in a major downsizing in the City. This was the post-big bang era when some financial services organisations had out-reached themselves and needed to make cutbacks. My abiding memory of this exercise is the desire of the consulting team to deliver a thoroughly professional service for the client and the individuals impacted by the exercise. In truth there is no easy way to make someone redundant; it's probably the most diffi-cult thing most managers have to do.

We used to share war stories about the ways in which the news was conveyed. In one case, a salesman was instructed to ensure he had some spare cash with him for a meeting with his boss. He was made redundant at a motorway service station and told to find his own way home, having to leave his company car. Others drew attention to messages by fax and tannoy. These days e-mail may provide the means for those organisations unwilling to treat their employees appropriately. As this book was in progress, the football manager Gus Poyet apparently discovered his services were no longer required by his club via the BBC, for whom he was covering a football tournament.

Quite apart from the impact on the people made redundant by such inadequate means, the effect on the remaining workforce isn't great either. Indeed this is the moment at which some indi-viduals decide it's time to move on. If this is the situation you are experiencing, do take the time to reflect very carefully on the best way forward for you using the tools outlined in the text. Your future may still be with your current employer, at least in the short term. More enlightened employers will adopt the notion of the "good leaver", aiming to treat their people with dignity and other support.

It is for the latter reason that outplacement has grown considerably over the last twenty years. For those who have not come across the term, it is the structured process by which those who have lost their jobs are provided with support to help them come to terms with what has happened followed by a range of modules, courses and talks that generally focus on themes such as:

- 'Taking Stock' – assessing where you are now, getting started on the next step in your career journey, identifying and building on your strengths

- 'Creating Choices' – identifying what you want to achieve, designing an effective CV, preparing for selection, assessments and interview processes

- 'Tools and Tactics' – how to market yourself, sources of jobs, using networking to source possible jobs

As well as wishing to fulfil their obligation to redundant employees, many organisations also recognise that employee engagement initiatives will fail if former employees struggle to find jobs. Outplacement may also form part of the organisation's retention strategy, recognising that, at times of significant change, their best workers may seek to have control over their career and jump ship first.

It is debatable that the outplacement industry may have peaked. Employers are increasingly cost conscious and consequently may be reducing the range of services they are prepared to pay for. These have typically been tiered depending on the status of the individual and the speed with which they were likely to be able to re-enter the labour market. The base programme might cover the themes described above with a mixture of group and individual-based support with more senior post holders offered extended one-on-one support. There is a distinct market for senior people with both a wider range of offerings and considerable flexibility in both content and the duration of support.

In the wider market some outplacement providers have been a little like factory farmers, responding to a limited budget and reducing their offering to the lowest common denominator with little flexibility. In the last five years or so, there has been a marked shift to "virtual" outplacement, which offers the employer significant reductions in cost but also a considerable diminution of the time available – if any – for face-to-face contact.

Michael Moran, Chief Executive of 10Eighty, a career and talent management consultancy, has significant experience in this field and notes that lowering costs is not the only driver: "Over the last decade, people and organisations have become used to redundancy. This does not minimise the importance of providing support and in some areas technology has produced a win-win with psychometric reports completed on line freeing up time for face-to-face discussion on interpreting the results. Equally, the introduction of e-learning has given job searchers access to a wide range of sophisticated databases and job boards."

Michael also observes that: "Very few people pay for their own outplacement and probably spend more time planning their next holiday than reflecting on how best to manage their career. Career management is for life, not just in times of outplacement."

The questions below are the ones you need to ask to better understand what you may be about to receive. You may be pleasantly surprised at the ways in which your programme could be adapted to your needs. And never say "no" to outplacement! Some people are very upset at losing their job, so much so that they want to distance themselves from their employer as fast as possible, and outplacement is something they can assert control over by refusing it: not a good idea.

Key questions to ask your employer:

- Is there a choice of providers?

- If I don't like them may I use the budget with another provider?

- How will the programme be structured?

You need clarity from both your employer (the paymaster) and the outplacement provider to ensure there are no surprises. For the outplacement provider, key questions are:

- How would my programme be structured?

  - Discovering the balance between one-to-one work and group sessions is important

  - How many hours do I have? Does this include face-to-face, telephone and internet support?

- May I meet some former participants?

  - People who have recently completed the programme and found a new role are very useful sources of feedback

- Am I able to choose who will help me?

  - Empathy makes a difference, but also think about who will best be able to help and stretch you

  - Their background and its relevance to your needs – e.g. sector or functional knowledge

  - Their "success" rate

- Their style of support

- How much flexibility will I have?
  - For example, could you substitute more help with your market research on potential employers with a workshop on setting up your own business
  - You may wish to postpone starting the programme; is the programme of fixed and limited duration, e.g. fixed at three months from the start date, or more flexible with the meter stopped when you wish to pause?

- What resources and services will be available to me?
  - Work station availability
  - Access out of normal office hours
  - Research expertise available to you
  - Clerical support

A good outplacement provider will only use professionally accredited consultants and will quality control its own processes. However, the nature of the business model adopted to cope with the ups and downs of different sectors of the economy does mean that a significant proportion of these people may be associates rather than full timers. This is of itself not a problem; it is if the continuity of the support you require is disrupted.

There is a distinct niche market for senior people who have been made redundant with a small number of excellent providers who will accept people they feel they will be able to place, rather than take your money whatever your likelihood of future employment. You will get a wider range of support and an in-depth opportunity to review yourself and also to receive feedback from those you have worked with. There is also a range of other providers who will hawk your CV around various search firms and not a lot more, so do your due diligence carefully and shop around with care.

If buying your own outplacement is economically not viable there are a variety of ways forward. One would hope this book will reduce your need to get a third party to prepare your CV; there seems to have been a mini boom in those offering this service. As you will have gathered from this book, the preference here is for personal ownership of your CV; the more time and energy you give it, the more you will benefit. The thing no one should do is to boilerplate phrases gleaned from the many sites online with tips on how to secure your next job. I once interviewed an individual who possessed about 10% of the capability alleged in their CV! The next chapter explores how you can avoid this trap.

A CEO who benefitted from outplacement on two occasions observed that: "The process imposed a very useful discipline on me, keeping me focused and on the right track. Particularly valuable were the suggestions on how I could increase my market visibility. The provider also gave me a safe environment in which to see myself as an interviewer sees me, using role plays and CCTV. The research person was very good as was the facility to have someone to take my messages." This individual also emphasised the need for clarity as to what you want, not from the outset but as a result of the outplacement process, commenting that search firms "can only handle one proposition at a time so don't confuse them – they are generally not careers advisers".

An interesting comment was the need for outplacement providers to keep reminding their clients that: "They won't get you the job – you will; they can make a big difference but you must put the energy into building and using your own network."

They also reiterated the importance of working with a provider which has consultants with industry experience at an appropriate level of seniority.

The employer perspective

Providing outplacement support also sends a powerful message to those who see other colleagues lose their jobs; it shows that their employer is doing the best they can and helps to reassure "survivors" who may be unsettled and, not unreasonably, fearful of what the future holds for them. It is more important than ever to safeguard the talent you will need when the business climate improves.

Executive coaching

Executive coaching can offer benefits at a number of pinch points in your career journey ranging from working with a coach on a one-to-one basis or as part of the outplacement process to get you back to work; providing mid-career support on the options available and the choices required; and during the first few months of a new role where challenges in assimilation and delivering results can derail an individual.

Before exploring the areas where the coaching process has value in the context of **ROM**, let us first take a look at executive coaching more generally. My own working definition is that it is "the focused application of skills and wisdom that deliver performance improvement through robust support and challenge". What's required is a coach able to support a collaborative and practically focused process which is empathetic and individually concentrated. Frequently the goals are centred on supporting and accelerating the participant's capability to:

• Improve performance or behaviour

• Maximise potential

• Develop skills

• Achieve personal fulfilment

• Differentiate between reality and perception

The backdrop against which the support of the coach is valuable typically includes:

The process is increasingly individuals, teams and organisations face challenges; especially during times of transition and change:

• New roles ranging from a new job in a new organisation to an international transfer or leading a new function

• Preparing for, and responding to, the consequences of merger and acquisition

• Delivering and leading organisational change

• Leading, sponsoring and managing complex projects

This is achieved through a programme of structured conversations over an agreed period of time using a range of reflective processes and tools to address agreed goals – typically between six to 12 sessions of between two to three hours duration over a six-month period. An effective programme provides the opportunity to review yourself, your choices and needs in a safe environment. The process provides focus and support and constructive challenge. The self-awareness that participants gain is a major benefit. Understanding that "potential minus interference equals performance" is important.

Our own perceptions – and awareness – of "interference" can significantly detract from the achievement of our full potential. Frequently "interference" is related to a lack of clarity and understanding of roles, boundaries and accountability. As organisations have become more complex maybe we should not be too surprised at this. Nonetheless, individual responses to apparent contradictions in these three areas can lead to personal disengagement or increased friction in the workplace, to the detriment of one's performance.

An interesting – and useful – way of checking on your sense of clarity of your current job is to draw a representation of your own accountabilities and interactions with the rest of the team, function and organisation. This is not a test of your artistic skills or a test of anything else. It is an opportunity to describe your working situation in a different way, exercising a different part of your brain. Ideally explain what you have created to a friend. They don't need to be too knowledgeable about your role, the real power is what you notice as you describe what you have drawn. You may be surprised at the insights this provides!

Organisations increasingly look to executive coaching to provide impetus to high potential people. It may be that your own conversations with your employer have led to the offer of support in the form of coaching. It is important to be clear about roles: the participant owns, the coach guides, and the sponsor supports the process. The focus is to enable the participant to review and ultimately own solutions to the issues upon which they seek resolution. The coach acts as sparring partner in a neutral environment which provides a safety net within which to play with ideas and test assumptions. Without clarity on roles, the risk is the process will fall into a "Bermuda Triangle" lacking purpose and energy.

Here is an example of the terms of reference for a middle manager in a support function in a manufacturing business:

- To create a space within which to review what moving to the next stage of your career with the company will look like.

- To review team management, including making enough time, and saying "no".

- Getting more insight into management tools and processes including ways of reviewing the strengths and weaknesses in a team.

- Review approaches to making the step up from being an information provider to taking the lead in making the case for, and driving change in the business.

- Look at ways of presenting information/new ways of working/selling the vision to management in written and verbal formats.

As with outplacement there are a number of questions you will wish to ask your potential coach, just as they will wish to ensure the "coachability" of those they choose to work with. The latter point includes the participant being clear about making the time for their coaching sessions. Clearly business issues sometimes lead to a session being cancelled, but the key driver is commitment to the coaching process. Unfortunately you cannot compress all your coaching sessions into one weekend event and expect a useful outcome!

Bearing in mind the reality that executive coaching is an unregulated profession, the organisation will need to be satisfied that prospective coaches:

- Are appropriately qualified and members of a recognised coaching organisation

- Have experience of operating at senior level

- Have a flexible approach

- Demonstrate the capacity to focus on the individual whilst understanding the wider corporate context

- Recognise the importance of a structured "ending" to each programme and do not develop a dependency relationship on the part of the participant

- Consider their own continuous professional development

Both the organisation and the potential participant will be interested in:

- How the coach works

  - A typical session

  - Face to face supported by telephone support?

  - What psychometrics do they typically use?

  - How they feedback progress to the organisation whilst maintaining the confidentiality of the sessions

- What work experience did they have before training as an executive coach?

- What is a typical assignment?

- What do they feel makes a coaching relationship effective?

- How are they able to be both supportive and challenging?

- Their demonstration of interpersonal skills: listening, questioning and providing feedback

Reflect on how they come across as a "whole" person with the capacity to enrich understanding with anecdotes and appropriate use of models; their personal values; the "buzz" they get from coaching; and the range of skills they are able to deploy including humour, compassion, empathy, curiosity and an understanding of your own situation. Finally, do you trust them as someone with whom you will be able to work?

Individuals who feel their career is at risk of stalling may ask their organisation for support in the form of coaching or hire a coach on a personal basis, as may redundant managers. The issues and questions discussed earlier remain relevant.

There is also an important ethical issue here since an executive coach engaged by the organisation has to maintain the confidentiality of all their conversations with the participant. A positive outcome for some participants is the confidence the process gives them to open up to their boss on issues that may be troubling them. The role of the coach is to support them, not act on their behalf as a surrogate communicator. There is one exception to this, namely if the coach fears the individual is "in harm's way" when they would need to alert the organisation to their concerns. This is a very rare occurrence. More likely is a misunderstanding on the part of the participant that the coach is there to help them get out of the organisation. Generally coaches are hired to help the individual and the organisation get the best from each other. They are not engaged on the organisation's behalf to persuade the participant by stealth to seek redundancy. If the process is aimed at helping an individual's move away from the organisation this must be explicitly recognised by all parties at the outset and reflected in the terms of reference.

By way of a "lighter" perspective on coaches, note the following:

Coaches to avoid

The motto "buyers beware" applies to any purchase. The types of coach identified below are rare, but they do sometimes emerge from the shadows:

The trophy coach

"We think you've reached a point in your career where a coach would be of great help. As you probably know, a number of very senior managers here have coaches." Is this potential recipient being rewarded or punished? Certainly having your own coach is the modern-day equivalent of having the keys to the executive cloakroom in some corporate circles. It may be apocryphal but the story of the City traders, who were lamenting the need to accept a coach without which they would not be considered for promotion, will resonate with many.

The coach as "collector"

Prepared to work within the organisation for anyone who will have him/her. There are limits to the number of participants one coach can effectively work with in one organisation without compromising ethics, boundaries and confidentiality.

The coach as surrogate manager

Your boss tells you: "As you know, I'll be away on secondment for the next six months. Don't worry; a chap from a coaching outfit has been hired to give you some help if you need it."

The adhesive coach

This individual tends to emphasise how expert they are. They alone are able to help you: "Never mind the chemistry, just trust me."

The coach on the couch

The coach on the couch offers huge amounts of empathy but little positive help. Probably confusing intuition with judgement they will relive their experience through yours: "That's just what happened to me – here's what I did..."

The absentee coach

The absentee coach prefers to coach via the telephone rather than face-to-face. They see themselves as so phenomenally successful; you should consider yourself lucky to get even this.

The borderless coach

With little sense of boundaries or ethics, this type of coach blithely goes where others will not. Lacking technical training and experience, they are best avoided.

Mentoring

In my youth I was (briefly) employed by a major detergent manufacturer as a retail salesman. This was way before the internet and "just in time" procurement had yet to evolve. My fellow "reps" were incentivised to sell based on a consultative selling model. On my first visit to a large store of a now defunct chain,

I was sought out by the manager and was peremptorily ordered to "follow me". When we reached the store warehouse the reason for his mood was self-evident and his words have stuck with me: "When I've sold that XXXXing lot you can come back but not before!"

This was one of my early lessons in distinguishing wants from needs and also a warning about the impact of short-term incentives, since my predecessors certainly got what they wanted, namely a bigger monthly bonus. Looking back on this episode I feel a mentor would have helped me navigate the sometimes opaque world of the rep.

There is a wide range of literature illustrating the differences between mentoring and coaching with the key differences being the on-going longer-term nature of mentoring, usually with a more experienced/qualified colleague rather than an outsider. A colleague – moving to a new, more complex organisation – identified a more senior colleague who appeared to have the right qualities to be a mentor and asked for some help. The individual was pleased to be able to provide support in a number of ways including how best to make sense of the decision-making process within the business and introduce her to colleagues in other parts of the operation where there were potential opportunities for working collaboratively to develop new products and services. The relationship is working because "it is non-judgemental and our conversations are between the two of us and don't go any further".

Another individual's experience supports this perspective:

"In the first few days/weeks/months of joining a business or starting in a new role, a mentor can be instrumental in advising you/guiding you through the maze that is the corporate world. A good mentor will provide practical advice on who the movers and shakers in the organisation are and who to spend your time getting to know (and who to avoid). They will (if they believe/trust in you) open up their network to you and point you in the right direction of who to speak with, often opening doors quickly for you by authorising you to 'mention my name when you call'. Good mentors are the wise owls in the organisation. They are there to turn to for advice and guidance when you hit the inevitable bumps in the road. When things go well, your mentor relationship will turn to a "sponsor" relationship: Have you seen the great work that x is doing? and raise your profile with senior stakeholders in the business. For me, having a well-chosen mentor is an absolute must. The key is to keep the mentor relationship for a short period of time where the mentor can add the maximum amount of value to you, turn them into a sponsor and move on."

The steps	Self-Management	Processes
Mapping	Balancing Focus & Desire	Feedback and the Performance Review
Planning		
Exploring	Insight	Outplacement, Executive Coaching and Mentoring
Demonstrating Competence		
Arriving & Delivering	Connecting	My Big Fat CV
Consolidating & Reviewing		

The Takeaway

However good those who help and advise you are, you are the owner of the processes they deliver.

Chapter Six
My Big Fat CV

"Don't confuse a career with a life."

Hillary Rodham Clinton

This chapter is the one which can potentially make the biggest difference to your capacity to take ownership of your career and your **ROM**. You need a CV, but not any old CV. You need My Big Fat CV (MBFCV). This idea will run counter to much of the advice you may have received. However, the payoff will be considerable so please read on and stay energised.

Why this matters

This step will appear counter intuitive and many readers will respond to this suggestion with deep cynicism! That's because you perceive the CV as a "dead" document which records the past or feel that an employer or agency really need to meet you in person rather than rely on your CV. Unfortunately these days your CV is the prime document that will get you through most doors! There are organisations and individuals who will – for a fee – write your CV for you, so why not use them and spend the time saved on other activities? Not a great idea unless you are coached through the process of developing your own CV. The very real risk is that a document that you have not created will not represent you accurately and neither might you live up to it.

The process of creating the document we will now refer to as MBFCV is the precursor to the short, focused documents you will subsequently utilise to get yourself on the radar of recruiters, search firms and potential employers. The reason for laying such emphasis on MBFCV is to help you overcome a number of traps which can derail your search for a new role. These include:

- Poorly presented CVs which do nothing to differentiate the sender from other candidates

- Preparing the document in haste with little focus on the expectations of the reader or the needs of the organisation

- Short selling yourself by failing to describe your achievements in an appropriate manner

- Failing to see the benefits of taking the time to prepare a core CV which will showcase your successes and achievements and dramatically enhance your performance at interview

We explore the issue of being ring ready or ring rusty in terms of interview expertise a little later in Chapter Eight. For the moment be aware that however good your track record, if you are unable to present this in an articulate, focused and responsive manner at an interview you are unlikely to be successful.

The process underpinning the creation of your own MBFCV is one which will connect your feelings and memories with your aspirations. It's not difficult but will take a few days to both trawl your memory for the information required and allow yourself time to reflect on what you are recalling. This will raise your awareness on a number of levels, supporting your capacity to respond more effectively to the interview questions that sometimes cause us to stumble.

Your MBFCV will enable you to:

- Develop an accurate record of your employment history

- Record the information you need to illustrate qualitative and quantitative elements of your achievements to date

- Explore what you liked and disliked about each of your jobs and employers

- Better understand "where am I now and how did I get here?"

- Understand the past and present of your career and contribute to more effective identification of expectations for the future

Structure

What's needed is as much detail as you can marshal on your career to date. Anyone who suggests the first step is to create a "short, compelling CV" is selling you short.

One way to view this is as if you have hired a biographer to write your work history encompassing your career ambitions, fulfilling roles and thwarted ambitions. It's also much easier to prune a long document and refocus it depending on need than to create a bespoke version from scratch when under pressure.

There are a few ideas below to provide some structure to the process, but do not be too concerned about format. Essentially what is needed is a big "dump" of what you've done, when you did it, for whom and the outcomes you achieved. The process will help you to recall issues, events and successes that you have long forgotten. In the context of the characteristics of effective career managers this process will connect you to your career highlights, along with the lows, and provide insight into your expectations and ambitions as your career has progressed. By reassembling the information in this way you will acquire renewed knowledge of yourself and quite possibly a new perspective on some of your career choices. At this stage we are developing as full a picture as possible, so here's your opportunity to be as honest with yourself as you are able. This process is not an instant fix, so give yourself time to do this thoughtfully and thoroughly.

None of us will approach this in the same way, so taking a perspective that has both breadth and depth is important; having a helicopter view is great but you also need to get a real feel for the terrain you will be marching over. It is of fundamental importance to take time to do this properly. As someone who used to detest creating a new version of my own CV, no doubt I now have the zeal of any convert but please bear with me.

The positive trade-off of making this investment is the time it will save you later when you need a CV for a particular role. The time saved by not doing a substandard job on an already poor CV to meet a deadline will give you time to review more fully what the employer or agency is really looking for. If you were in their shoes what would differentiate one candidate's experience from another? I was recently told about a candidate who failed to get through the selection process to the interview stage. The individual asked for feedback, which was given, and it emerged that the candidate did indeed appear to have the specific experience required. However, for whatever reason, this was not included in their application and they failed to get through the first stage of the selection process. Never make the assumption that someone will "read between the lines" and see you anyway.

Hopefully you are now persuaded that your MBFCV is worth the effort. The minimum information is indicated in the template below. Some of this information is factual; some is more judgmental. For the factual material, depending on your age and experience this may require a little research to assemble the information. Paradoxically, if most of your career has been with one organisation, albeit one in which you have successfully progressed over the years, the need to develop any form of CV may have proven unnecessary. It may also be enlightening to discover the total value of your current reward and benefits package, particularly important if your package includes a final salary pension.

The item asking for information on training, learning and observation is to record events, team building or awareness gained from undertaking psychometric assessments. This is an area often neglected when people leave an employer. You may still have the handouts from a course or the report from a personality inventory, but have you ever opened them? These are well worth another look. Remember that these are not "test" results; they provide a perspective based on your responses to a range of questions. Consequently they are derived from your answers to a questionnaire rather than observation based. Nonetheless many of these instruments give a valuable insight into strengths and deficits and one's default under pressure. Unfortunately some organisations adopt a sheep dip to the use of these instruments with insufficient one-on-one feedback, hence the likelihood that many reports languish on the shelf. If you've completed a few of these you may see a consistent pattern emerging, which provides a useful basis for soliciting feedback from others.

Recall courses, development programmes and learning, skills and qualifications acquired. Wherever possible identify what difference these events made to you in terms of self-awareness and performance. In particular, what you did differently and how you deployed the knowledge gained. A useful way to do this is to focus on:

- What you took away from team events in the shape of new ideas, skills or self-awareness

- What you learned from clients

- Contributions to your industry, sector or function through:

    - Talks or speeches

    - Articles in the trade or national press

    - Interviews

    - Press comment or interviews

    - Conference attendance and presentations

    - Industry groups and networks including active involvement in branch activities

Education or employer: nature of the business or organisation:	
Dates of employment:	
Job title:	
Level or grade:	
Reported to:	
Direct reports:	
Indirect reports:	
Why you took the job	
Key accountabilities and deliverables with quantifiable measures of success	
People, equipment and assets under your direct control	
Your pay, benefits and pension package	
Reason for leaving	
Describe your proudest moment in this job	

Describe what you feel was your biggest challenge	
Describe the most important lesson you learned in this job	
Describe what you really enjoyed	
Describe what you least liked	
Which word best describes your relationship with the organisation?	Adversarial Fulfilling Comfortable Challenging
Which word best describes your relationship with your boss?	Friendly Professional Acrimonious Stressful
Which word best describes your relationship with your team?	Harmonious Remote Rewarding Difficult
Training, development and learning: what difference did it make to your behaviour and performance?	

The final step is to identify each and every example of successes and positive outcomes achieved against the odds. It is very important to be able to illustrate the difference you made, so pay particular attention to illustrating outcomes with quantifiable and/or qualitative measures and the context within which these actions were taken, e.g. a business turnaround, operational improvement programmes or a major project. Also reflect on what you have learned from failure and what you have changed as a result. This will stand you in good stead when we move onto the development of a work-related CV in Chapter Eight.

If you have completed the MBFCV in one go, or during the course of one weekend, that's a little too fast. You need to let the process take over and allow memories, achievements, failures and feelings to surface. Each time this happens, do make a quick note to remind yourself to add these items to the document.

When the time seems right to you, please move on...

Making sense of your MBFCV

Whether you have had one job or a variety in one organisation or many, having completed these summaries you will have very likely experienced many feelings about what worked, what didn't and what you liked and what may have bored or failed to stimulate you. You may be reflecting that you should never have left a prior employer or are more certain that you need to make a move. This could be for many reasons:

- The nature of the job, e.g. too much routine/too little structure

- The culture of the organisation

- The relationship with your boss

- The location

- The journey to work

- Promises made at interview not kept

- Challenges at home

- No opportunity to develop yourself

You have also probably reminisced about people you have not thought about for some time. Now is the time to collate all these names and check out where they are now. You may well discover they are potentially of great use as a means of widening your network.

The simple questions about relationships may have triggered more feelings than anticipated. These frequently fall into the categories of:

Performance – how did I do? And how did your team and the organisation fare? You may have delivered against the odds; been a member of a team going through a difficult period of transition; or worked for a leader in an organisation which brought out the best in you.

Pride – your proudest moment? This may not be delivering a record-breaking sales target, it could be seeing one of your colleagues benefit from your guidance.

People – your biggest fans and your most difficult customers? Sometimes recalling people you have worked with can produce a sense of loss; the key is to understand what made these times so memorable.

Prospects – were you expecting a major career change? Did it happen? What you expected at the time and how you view things now may be a little different. If your expectations were not met, consider all the factors that may have been at work including your own behaviour.

Projects – involvement with projects and their outcomes? Many people take their experience working on projects for granted. This may be because projects are now such a common facet of organisational life. However, involvement with projects will have given you both experience and insight. A project that failed to deliver all that was expected may still have given you a significant insight into the factors that determine success.

Your responses to the questions on relationships may well need a little fleshing out. One's immediate response to an organisation which you have recently involuntarily left may be somewhat harsh. Equally, time and distance can distort memories of a former role so take your time to check out how you really feel.

The clusters above are, of themselves, not good or bad. A role which is described as "challenging, stressful and remote" may have been a fantastic learning experience, where you were given accountability for a unit with little contact with your line boss. An environment which is/was "comfortable, friendly and harmonious" may have prevented an individual fulfilling their full potential and given them little in the way of employability for the longer term. A high salary may have compensated for other challenges.

What were you expecting when you took the job in the first place? What are the differences between your expectations and your current perception of your relationships telling you? Of course, at this point we only have your own perception of these relationships. This is valuable, but is only a partial view. A reality check is now called for to test out what you have learned from this process and whether you have a clearer sense of what an ideal role would potentially need to provide, including:

- The degree of stretch or comfort you would appreciate

- The type of culture you feel best suits you

- The way you prefer to work and be managed

Take the time to see if there are patterns of issues that are related to your enjoyment of a particular job and success in it. It's at this point that some of us will make some irrevocable choices about what to do next. One respondent described their most important career choices as being:

- Accidentally joining the police

- Staying within the uniform branch to match my skills and inclinations

- Seeking promotion

- Leaving the police to see what else would appear

- Taking a role based on salary and no due diligence about the company – this was a huge mistake

- Taking on a role in the voluntary sector that promised more fulfillment

- Realising that I had "run out of steam" in my current job, deciding to leave and explore new possibilities

- Based on this experience their advice to others is to:

- Always check out the environment/context you are trying to enter

- Apply for jobs that suit your skills and ethos

- Be clear how important the money is (or is not)

- Be self-aware

- Accept that success may not always arrive through the first opportunity

Another respondent reflected that: "After graduation, joining a large bank's generic graduate training scheme was important for a negative reason. It made me realise that I did not wish to work in a large bureaucratic organisation in what was, at that time, a very male-dominated industry. I learned a lot from that mistake."

This can potentially be a lonely space and of fundamental importance is the need to understand your patterns of behaviour when confronting the unknown. Do you tend to take refuge in the detail or the big picture? This book will help you understand the importance of both these perspectives and the more you expand your network the more you will benefit.

The Takeaway

Take the time to focus on developing a heavyweight My Big Fat CV. It will provide a great basis for job-related CVs and significantly improve your recall of achievements, likes and dislikes. Most importantly it will help you understand what you really want from your career.

Chapter Seven
Mapping and Planning

"It was ...disconcerting to examine your charts before a proposed flight only to find that in many cases the bulk of the terrain over which you had to fly was bluntly marked 'UNSURVEYED'."

Beryl Markham, *"West with the Night"*

This chapter looks at the importance of mapping and planning to avoid the risk of accidentally straying into unsurveyed territory.

Mapping

The good news is that a substantial amount of your mapping will have been completed as you developed your MBFCV and subsequently reviewed the themes, patterns, likes and dislikes that emerged from your career journey. This will have given you a perspective on where you are and what you have achieved. There are qualitative and quantitative aspects to this and some of the preceding work will have reinforced or challenged what you would regard as your "worth". However, worth is derived from a range of sometimes conflicting sources, opinions and actions. It certainly should not be directly derived from your pay package or time with the organisation, although these may sometimes contribute to a referred worth which may under or overstate your achievements. There are a number of factors to consider:

- Reputation
  - What do others say about you; how supportive are your referees? What do your boss, function head or Non-Executive Directors (NEDs) think of you?

- Scarce skills
  - Can be useful, but can impede progress. You may be very well paid for your expertise and consequently lose out on opportunities to widen your repertoire or choose to "take the money whilst it's available". For example are you one of a select few programmers specialising in very aged software? This may make you worth a lot in a diminishing market. Or are you experienced in an area of work undergoing a boom or renaissance? Examples include Solvency II in the insurance industry, US GAAP in accounting, and environmental and energy expertise.

- Delivery and track record
  - Are you associated with a successful organisation or one that has recently faltered or failed? Depending on seniority there may be a positive halo impact or guilt by association.
  - What have you got to show for your time with the organisation?
  - Do you have a CV which demonstrates achievement?
  - What career headroom do you require? Are you comfortable taking your chances and waiting for the next opportunity to present itself, or do you need to operate in an apparently more structured environment?

- You may currently be working for the organisation from hell – it does happen. Review what led you to join the organisation in the first place. What does this tell you about yourself?

• Social and workplace capital

- How well are you networked? Virtual and actual networks are extremely useful for highlighting your expertise, researching potential employers and sounding out ideas. Professional networks are a significant source of potential candidates for some search firms.

- How many search firms or recruiters are you in regular contact with?

• Job size

- These days there are significant differences in pay between sectors for jobs of apparently the same size. You need to show the scale and impact of the resources you have been managing to ensure that your capability will be fairly benchmarked. If you are attempting to move out of a low paying sector, your accountabilities and results must be clearly stated and understandable with sufficient detail to gain attention.

• Job title

- This can dramatically influence individuals, with a step to a CEO role being their dream job, even in a very small operating unit. Without P&L (profit and loss) experience this will be a challenge. Your reporting line and the assets/resources under your control are relevant.

• Market value

- Recruitment agencies and search firms frequently produce reports on salary trends which are used as marketing collateral but are also very often available online and will give you an insight into sector and market trends.

- Peer comparison

  - Ranking yourself against classmates or colleagues is, of itself, not that useful; seeking their ideas is.

- Derived from your current employer

  - Time with blue chip employers potentially commands respect.

- What difference did you make?

  - Can you show this with conviction and energy?

The challenge now is to identify lines of best fit in terms of the job, the organisation and the location of your next job. This is the final stage of mapping and the first stage of planning.

As a starter ask yourself:

- What do you feel you are really good at?

  - What evidence is available to support this feeling?

- In planning for the future, is there anything you want to avoid?

  - What makes you feel this?

- How have your ambitions changed as your career has progressed?

  - What do you feel caused these shifts?

- What are you particularly looking forward to?

  - What underpins this?

- What will you need to do to make this happen?

- Is this achievable?

• What are your key life goals over the next ten years?

- How different are they to your current goals?

• What about your career goals over the same period?

- What will success look like?

What you do **not** want to do may sometimes be clearer than that which attracts you. Consequently as you move from the mapping step to that of planning and exploring you will need to keep an open mind as to whether you need to recalibrate your goals. General Eisenhower is often quoted as commenting that, "Plans are useless but planning is essential." The key thing about the initial plan is that it sets the start point from which you are able to track changes, whether self-imposed or in response to surprises or new information.

Planning

Your plan needs to consider the following factors before objectives can be set.

When?

We have already explored the dangers of taking immediate action without an action plan. Resigning with nowhere to go may not be the best course of action; it is certainly more difficult to gain a new job than walk out on one. Your availability will be affected by your notice period or the duration of any gardening leave. There may also be financial considerations including the size of any severance payments and the point at which you will need your earnings flow to resume. Will some form of part-time or consulting work be required to mitigate loss of earnings whilst looking for a full-time position?

You also need to plan how you will use your time as you look for your next role and track the actions you are taking. Some of us are very structured; for those who are not, a plan is essential to ensure you make the best use of your time and maintain an appropriate level of activity. If you are comfortable with a structured approach, do not lose sight of the possible need to flex your plan as opportunities or unexpected obstacles arise.

Where?

"I'll go where the work is" needs to be underpinned by a clear understanding of the economic implications. A move to the countryside may result in a long – and costly – commute to work. The economic consequences of an international assignment also need careful calibration. Issues such as housing allowances and school fees will need to be clarified. Moreover, what will happen at the end of the assignment? The choices available at the start of the assignment may have disappeared by the end of your time away. Re-entry is often more challenging than your first few months in a new location and culture, since the changes at your "home" location may have been considerable during your absence. Once again, throughout your assignment you must be prepared to be proactive in maintaining existing networks within the organisation as well as forging new ones.

Mode?

This may be the ideal time to start your own business, go part time or seek a NED role. Maybe you are financially secure enough to take a break to consider your future or are you considering returning to education as a mature student? If your current employer is paying for part-time study or professional qualifications, will a new one support the costs and time required in the same way?

The interim market has expanded dramatically over the last decade and can be a very fulfilling route. However, it is not for everyone and you would almost certainly need to set yourself up as self-employed. There are a number of specialist interim recruiters who could be a good source of advice. Interim roles come in many shapes and sizes these days and do sometimes mutate into permanent roles. However the challenge of looking for your next role on a regular basis may offset the flexibility and enjoyment of being able to "work when I wish".

What?

What exactly do you expect to be doing? This can range from a similar job in a new location to a significant step into a leadership role. Or are you aiming to transfer your functional skills to a new sector. Your next move does not have to be to a "bigger" role; it could be a similar role in a smaller organisation or a sideways move.

How?

Without a thorough understanding of yourself and the labour market you significantly weaken your chances of success. Equally, without exploring alternatives you may ignore the optimal choices available to you at this point in your career. Unfortunately this is not a science; your own perceptions and values along with those of a recruiter, search firm or employer all play their part. The feedback you have gathered about yourself and the on-going development of your network and your networking skills are very important determinants of success.

Collateral?

How will you market yourself to the people who may be able to market you? Your MBFCV now needs to be used to form the basis for a great CV.

Package?

You need to be clear with yourself about the package you desire and consider very carefully the minimum package required. You need to give this very careful thought, taking into account your likely "market value". This is an area where elephant traps may undo an individual who has a clear view of their own worth, but may not understand the reward structure of other organisations. If your search firm has a strategic relationship with the organisation in question you are more likely to be given a steer not only of the package on joining but also the organisation's track record of accelerating the progress of proven high potential employees. This is a situation where a firm with trusted adviser status can be extremely useful to both candidate and client.

For senior jobs, another issue may be the cost of foregoing the potential gains from membership of current Long-Term Incentive Plans and cost to a new employer of ensuring you are not worse off by making the move.

Prospects?

Is this a long-term career move or a short-term shift into a project role where your skills will command a high daily rate? Or are you looking for an opportunity to work pro bono for a not-for-profit organisation?

Culture and operating style?

Patterns of behaviour do have a habit of repeating themselves. Use your MBFCV to focus on what you've really enjoyed and been successful at, and factor in the feedback you have been given. As your job hunt progresses, research and if possible speak to people in your chosen organisations. Your due diligence will need to explore the organisation's structure along with the role and boundary implications of the job you are applying for.

Why?

It may be self-evident to you, but take the time to revisit the rationale for any move and identify the alternatives. The stress test below will build on this.

It can be difficult to identify your future prospects if your business has been taken over. A recent report on private equity buyout and subsequent performance drives this point home with the authors (Professor Geoffrey Wood, Warwick Business School, June 2013) suggesting that: "Imported financially focused management doesn't appreciate a firm's human assets and capabilities. Hence they are more likely to lay off staff and less aware of the consequences this may have for future performance."

If you are in this position and there has been little apparent effort to benchmark the skills and talent available in the newly acquired organisation, don't jump ship. But do investigate how the new owners are going to run the business and try to get a feel for what this will mean to your own career prospects.

What if?

Think the unthinkable! This has both up and downsides; there may be new market opportunities or are you taking more of a risk than you might have realised with an organisation that has been downsizing its operations. The key thing is to validate your actions as far as possible by research and discussions with recruiters and search firms.

Stress test

A theme running throughout this book is the belief that good as we may be as managers of our own careers, there are limits to how much any of us can actually do by ourselves. **ROM** is about the choreography of the process and this is a point at which choreographing the ideas and support of others is critical. So identify the people you trust to constructively challenge your rationale for the direction you are proposing to move in.

The plan

Although your plan is going to be a work in progress as you explore various options, it is important that you begin to refine what you need to do and the key criteria that underpin your choices. Here is an example of the principles that have guided someone currently occupying a senior role in the food industry:

I have almost always applied the following principles when looking at roles, opportunities and managing (to the extent I have) my career:

- Work for the best company you can

- Work for an organisation with the right cultural fit for you

- Work for the right person who is going to give you the experience and challenge you need

- Do things you enjoy

- Know yourself and be clear and honest about your strengths and weaknesses

- Be clear about what experience you need to gain in this and the next role

- Look for roles or experience that can constructively differentiate my CV from that of others

- Keep learning

With these observations in mind, the matrix below provides a straightforward means of clarifying your current preferences. Completing this matrix may bring clarity or raise a number of dilemmas and also illustrate both uncertainties and knowledge gaps. The matrix may not accommodate all of your own needs so add items as appropriate.

Issues	Action required	Importance Hi/M/Lo	Questions and dilemmas?
When?			
Notice period			
Earliest available			
Timeline for finding next position			
Financial considerations			
Where?			
Local			
Regional			
National			
Europe			
Global			
Mode?			
Full time			
Part time			
Interim			
Contract			
Job share			
Freelance			
Intern			
Non-executive			
Advisory			
Homeworking			
Pro bono			
Further education			
What?			
The job			
The level			
The sector			
How?			

Research			
Search			
Recruit			
Direct			
Referral			
Network			
Collateral?			
CV			
Reputation			
References			
Network			
Package?			
The minimum?			
The mix: • Base • Bonus • LTIP • Pension • Benefits • Relocation • Support for ongoing qualifications			
Prospects?			
Up and out			
Career ladder			
Stepping stone			
Intellectual capital			
Blue chip			
Preferred culture and operating style?			
Role			
Boundaries			
Accountability			
Why?			

What if?			
Stress test?			
Who to involve?			
Your plan?			
Essential		High	

There may well be a number of areas where your responses indicate more uncertainty than you expected. This is not that surprising since a chat by the coffee machine about "how bad things are" or over a drink about the need "to move on and up" are generally underpinned by emotion rather than understanding. You may also find yourself in a Catch 22 situation where you simply do not have enough information to make a choice. You may feel you do not even have enough information on whom to approach.

Some of these are known unknowns and some are unknown unknowns. The latter may be known to a search firm looking for an individual who is not on their list of "the usual suspects", which is what makes your focused marketing through networking so very important.

You may find the following helpful in challenging yourself to think the unthinkable. Brainstorm the forces at work in the areas that consistently come up as important to you, e.g. the law, insurance, project management, procurement, and identify the key pressures they are confronting now and in the near future. Examples are:

Political/regulatory

- Instability

- Environmental lobbying

- Global tax regimes

Economic

- Price competition

- Low interest rates

- Low consumer confidence

- Poverty/philanthropy

Social

- Unemployment

- Social unrest

- Mortality/morbidity/quality of life

Technology

- "More from less"

- Underexploited

- Poorly sponsored, badly managed projects

Organisational

- Diversity

- Talent strain

- Balancing growth and risk

- Offshoring and outsourcing

- Lack of opportunity

Based on your own sense of the forces at work in the jobs and organisations you see yourself targeting, put yourself in the position of the people hiring their talent of the future. Are there potentially interesting career options? How can you show your understanding of the challenges and opportunities they face and illustrate the skills and experience you would bring with you? And which elements of your experience and competency set are really relevant in tomorrow's environment and can add value both to yourself and future potential employer?

This opportunity testing need not be confined to future employers; testing what's possible against the reality of today's marketplace **and** identifying how to create future opportunities in your current employer is important too. It could be that your current organisation is about to move into a new field or market through an acquisition or the creation of a new business unit. So if you are currently on the inside of an organisation, check out where the organisation sees talent shortages since there may be opportunities to make progress in an area you have never considered.

There is a corollary to this, namely the limiting beliefs we may unconsciously hold and which may literally hold us back. For example: "I would never have contemplated any form of public sector role had the headhunter not been given my name as a potential source of other candidates." This is by no means uncommon; another individual moved from a senior retail role to a CEO position in the shipping industry.

Here is an example showing how someone went about: "Making the decision to leave a lethargic declining industry, to join one that was in the ascendancy and which had the dynamic change necessary to advance in the organisation."

What have been your most important career choices?

The most important, in terms of achieving my career goals, were forming a strategic plan to move away from

---

a technical engineering-based role to one that employed my engineering knowledge to commercial aspects; initially value design and later technical sales and general and financial management.

What made the choice(s) so important?

Technical roles are not considered to be of sufficient importance to many organisations and so rewards and advancement are limited. Particularly coming from a technical training, where security and safely are the watchwords, it does not come naturally to move away from the role you are familiar with. Reading *Who Moved My Cheese* (Dr Spencer Johnson, Vermilion) should be part of the school syllabus!

What criteria did you use to make your choice(s)?

Easy. Were they willing to pay me more; if so, they clearly appreciated my skills more than the current employer.

From whom did you seek advice on your intentions?

In all of my moves I have tried to talk to the employees and observe the working environment as internet research was not available until relatively late in my career.

Describe the outcome(s) (e.g. new job/new employer/change of career direction)

Each move that I made had an incremental change in the role as I sought to distance myself from the perception that I was fundamentally an engineer. However, once in a role, the fact that I had an engineering background could often gain respect.

How satisfied are you with the outcome(s)?

Very. I have had an exciting, challenging, varied and, ultimately, well-paid career

Looking back, do you feel there is anything you could have done differently; what has been your most significant learning from the experience?

Yes, I should have more self-confidence in my ability to "hack it" in a new environment and should have spent more time making and following a career strategy rather than thinking of each employment as a job, rather than the next step.

What is now required is a plan which draws on all your learning and feelings. You will need to ask yourself whether the plan is deliverable within the timescale you have set yourself and the resources that will be required to keep on track. Test out the plan with those you trust; ask them and yourself: "Is this manageable? What is the upside and what are the risks?"

As you draft your plan do not underestimate the actions required and the time it will take to accomplish them. It is all too easy to identify an objective such as "make contact with ten recruitment agencies and get a face-to-face meeting with each of them" when you are full of enthusiasm. The reality of actually arranging these meetings may, however, take more time – and persistence – than you anticipated. Rather than becoming depressed at your "failure", learn from your experience and regularly review and recalibrate the key elements of your plan incorporating the knock-on impact of any changes. It may be that you are not aware of key dependencies until you actually try to get your plan to work, but attempt to identify these as you begin to plan since this may alert you to a basic but important requirement! The "benefits realisation" column is important to both tracking progress and the opportunity it will provide to celebrate success as you move forward!

The example below gives an idea of what a narrative version of a plan may look like. This is not a corporate plan so use a style with which you are comfortable and include unanswered issues as a memory jogger.

Objectives	Benefits	Activity required	Dependencies	Benefits realisation: outcomes achieved	Target date
Research search firms and identify key people with pharmaceutical search accountability	Will widen my distribution network and give me the opportunity to talk through my experience and ambitions with firms close to the market	Identify and make contact with key people Ask my network for ideas on who to contact	My CV needs to be fit for purpose My research needs to identify a good fit with what I would like to do next and the technical/managerial disciplines and Companies they have as clients	Not yet achieved – but will be based on face-to-face meetings and success will be getting a second meeting to talk about current assignments	2 weeks from now
Increase my networking activity	Widen my contacts Give me more exposure	Join work related networks and alumni networks as a first step	Using this proactively What if people do not want to connect with me?	Actively following with short meetings/coffee with people I have re-connected with after some time	On-going - will add at least 5 each week

A brief excursion

By way of a short interlude before progressing, do you feel the need for a career break? Is now the right moment to take time off? As with everything else, insight and outsight are critical. Discovering yourself in the Gobi desert may seem a great idea; maybe not so useful when you are actually there.

Economic pressures mean that many of us have to recalibrate our view of retirement. Lifetime employment is starting to look as if it might really be just that! It's also clear that many people are reflecting on what they really want from life and work on a deeper level than ever before. With this in mind, we think it's time for a fresh look at the aims and outcomes of the gap year. Something that emerged in the 1960s as a rather wacky, pioneering approach to learning more about oneself as a young adult has now become the norm rather than the exception. It's a big industry and a gap year is a justifiable investment, or expensive entertainment, depending on your perspective. Certainly at a time when many parents are under increasing cost pressure, there needs to be a clear sense of what's involved – and expected.

The concept of a gap year, whether for rest and recreation, recharging batteries or learning new skills is an extremely valuable opportunity for adults of all ages...but, to get the outcome you want, some boundary management is a necessity. How much time have you got? A "gap" needn't be year – it could be a day a week over two years. And what's the impact on your family and your career?

The paradox is that without sufficient planning what seems a great idea – and potentially a life-changing experience – can fail to meet, let alone match expectations. The framework below aims to help potential "gappers" to better understand their motives and to gain additional clarity around what they really want. The typology below may act as a wake-up call to the dreamers and a brake on those whose default is to Just Do It!

Absconder – "I need to get to a place where I can reflect and take stock." Doesn't always get that far, and for a short while becomes:

The Happy Hippy – reliving a past that never really happened; after a month or so becomes:

The Unhappy Hippy aka The Drifter – uncertain of purpose, and not too certain how he/she got into this mess. As they become more gripped by the "GAP", likely to become more preoccupied with money and stress than ever before.

The Traveller – aims to embark on a journey to look, listen and learn through exploration of new cultures and renewing contact with those previously enjoyed. Can be very productive if based on firm foundations and for someone who knows their own limitations; a six-month Trans-African camping expedition is not for everyone… particularly immediately after a divorce, redundancy or other shock.

The Learner – wants to develop new skills, or to enhance old ones. Has thoroughly researched available programmes and has a budget! Vast opportunities available, but requires lots of self-discipline.

The Improver – stretch yourself and take your ambition to a new level. There may be less to talk about when you return, but self-improvement provides its own reward.

The Contributor – putting something back through voluntary work need not include travel, although there are now many opportunities to combine travel with volunteer work. Opportunities closer to home through charities provide endless scope to make a difference.

The Reformer – changing and campaigning – supporting a cause with time and or money.

The Builder – putting down foundations and stimulating growth. In some cases literally putting down foundations and building one's own home. This may also be the time when a hobby begins to emerge as a business opportunity or a second career.

The Adventurer – aims to get out there and enjoy things. Not to be confused with The Absconder, this individual is self-aware and has realistic expectations, and is much more likely to gain from the experience.

Pro bono work

It may well be that at various stages in our careers we see volunteering as an option, whether to "give something back" or to gain experience for a subsequent move into the NGO sector. Here is a charity CEO's view on the benefits and pitfalls:

Volunteering – free labour?

No organisation turns away volunteers willingly. The thought of individuals performing tasks that would otherwise have to be paid for is deeply attractive. Obviously charities like the National Trust and the thousands of charity shops up and down the country simply could not survive without such support. But is this the perfect business arrangement? Do volunteers cost nothing and does the profit equation come out in favour of the outfit they support? Is altruism directly related to value?

The answers to these questions depend on many things but mainly on the individual who volunteers. Firstly does that person bring the skills to the role that will be valued within the organisation and are they doing it for the right reason? Charities often attract people who feel strongly about the issue that the charity is trying to address. Such people are often emotionally connected to that issue and, to put it politely, may have lost their sense of perspective. A desire to help does not mean they will be good at counselling individuals, balancing the books, writing policies or dealing with those the organisation is trying to help. The organisation must know what it wants its volunteers to do and ensure the people they accept into what is, hopefully, a defined business model, can perform those tasks.

Will they then need training? Without understanding the organisational principles or strategy or even the local health and safety regulations, they may be more of a liability than an asset. Training costs money as does the "volunteer coordinator" who is often employed to manage this "free" resource.

The attitude of a volunteer can also be a concern. Does their provision of time and effort give them the right to not turn up without warning? It may be that they expect to be treated differently to paid employees as they are providing the charity with a favour. With that an expectation of deference, a freedom to whinge and a haphazard approach to the role may arise.

But volunteers can be, and are often, immensely valuable. Website designers, IT experts generally or someone prepared to stand in a dark, cold room to ensure visitors are welcome are worth their weight in gold – until they feel the time needed to work for you is impacting upon their personal and professional life. What is the exit strategy? If they leave, who fixes the website or would you have to close the cold, dark room and disappoint visitors or leave it open and see priceless objects make their way off in a different direction?

Pro bono work – "for good" this phrase appears to mean – is a further example of the offer of labour and skills for the benefit of the organisation. A good lawyer is hard to come by but a criminal expert may not be so good at addressing the concerns about the complex lease of your rented accommodation. These professionally qualified people may not always be available as they may have to earn money at the precise point when you need them to advise you. Profit generally takes precedence over the volunteering principle.

Trustees of charities are often the archetype of the volunteer. They have a responsibility to ensure the charity manages its finances successfully and complies with the charitable aims under which it was established. Before accepting an individual into this crucial role it may be necessary to ask some pertinent questions, some of which may even appear a little facetious, such as:

• Why are you doing this?

• What is your experience of this sector?

• What skills will you bring to this role?

• Will you turn up for meetings?

• Will you be available outside of meetings?

• Will you help raise money for the organisation?

• What is your expectation of the organisation?

• Is this simply an opportunity to enhance your CV?

• Will you take the hard decisions and accept responsibility?

• Will you get to know and support the staff?

Cynicism is a thread running through all the above but without volunteers many organisations would flounder, and flounder quickly. There is a cost and a downside to volunteers but the generosity, skills and support they provide can be immense. From counselling the Chief Executive who is struggling with a huge role and huge worries, to painting the office walls they allow the system to flourish. Certainly no charity would be as effective without them. Just don't think it's easy!

The Takeaway

The process of mapping and planning will give you significant insight into your motivations and expectations and underpins each and every career journey. Appendix B contains "At the Heart of Making a Decision" which explores ways of connecting with your feelings.

Chapter Eight
Exploring and Demonstrating Competence

"I have learned from my past mistakes, and I am sure I can repeat them exactly."

Peter Cook

This chapter provides an overview of the recruitment and selection process and the actions you need to take to get yourself in front of the people who can best help you.

I am continually surprised by the number of senior people who get edgy when informed that part of the selection process includes psychometric "tests". Indeed a few times I have been asked whether there is a "right" answer; more frequently whether I can give them some background on the psychometric in question. I do emphasise that these are not "tests", but another means to help determine an individual's likely response to the challenges leaders face. These concerns appear to be based on the assumption that the only tricky part of the process is the assessment, which ignores the reality that the entirety of the recruitment and selection process is geared to allowing your future employer to assess your capability, potential and "fit" with their organisation! So be very clear, an effective process should be putting you under scrutiny from a variety of perspectives using a range of tools and processes from the first time you make contact.

Another misconception is to see one's interview performance as the prime determinant of success – you've got to get to the interview stage before that can happen! This is probably because a poor interview sticks in the mind; invariably the candidate thinks "I should have done that differently", no doubt after a rejection. Sadly **interviewers** rarely perceive their deficiencies. I once attended a refresher workshop on interview skills where the most senior attendee assumed the role of "sponsor" to avoid taking part and consequently missed a great opportunity to get some (much-needed) feedback on their own skills. Although interviews can be the stuff of nightmares, familiarity with the process supported by practice will help you to evince the qualities you possess.

Technology has dramatically changed the way recruitment and selection operates. Telephone interviews, electronic communication and the increasing absence of any face-to-face feedback to candidates make it imperative to gain and retain the attention of those who may help you get your next job. Interestingly a sign of our times is "toxic online disinhibition" which, it is suggested, is the reason communication without eye contact, such as an online rejection, may potentially evoke anger from the recipient.

The web allows access to information on a particular organisation which enables today's job seekers to conduct due diligence to a level unimaginable a decade ago. Equally, employers are now able to check out candidates on social media sites to gain an insight into their particular lifestyle.

The question you may now have in mind is: "How do I get interviews with the people I need to see?" This is actually the second question you should ask and is predicated upon your response to the first: "What collateral do I need to get myself connected to the people who can get me these interviews?" This is going to be determined by:

- How well connected you are

- What differentiates you from other potential candidates

- Clarity about the jobs you seek and a good understanding of the intermediaries who can get you in front of employers

- A contact plan which is regularly reviewed

- A focused, achievement-oriented CV

Organisations are able to draw on a wide range of methods to find the talent they require, which is generally determined by the seniority of the post. In the public sector there are clear procedures governing transparency and posts will invariably be advertised.

Most of us will be familiar with the principal methods used and having assessed your own connectivity to the labour market in Chapter Three you will be aware of:

- Press advertising
  - National
  - Local
  - Trade press

- Job boards
  - Professional
  - Social

- Academic links
  - Careers service
  - Alumni networks

- Organisation
  - Website
  - Alumni networks
  - Employee referral schemes
- Search firms
- Recruitment agencies
- Word of mouth

As part of your own research it is essential to be familiar with all of these channels to ensure you are using the most appropriate means to achieve your goals. This is an area where outplacement providers have a wide range of expertise.

There are a number of issues you need to be alert to. In the past a recruitment agency may have been given a contract by the employing organisation. These days you will find a variety of agencies competing with each other to find suitable candidates. Take a look at a few job boards and you will see this with very similar, but slightly different descriptions for a particular post advertised by a number of agencies. Once upon a time the recruiter may have been retained on an exclusive basis, but this is now unlikely to be the case for roles beneath the senior management level. So your choice of agencies needs to take this into account: which seems the most likely to put you forward for the roles you seek; how forthcoming are they about their real views of your employability; and how good are their relationships with the organisations they recruit for?

You may be able to identify the organisation and decide to apply directly. If so, check with your network to see if anyone might be able to assist you. Generally these applications will be forwarded to the agency for initial filtering, so your challenge is to build good relationships with the people at a number of agencies to help them to help you. The reality is that this very much depends on the location and your level of expertise combined with the roles they are actively hiring for right now. Rather than send an email, visit the offices in person and ask for a conversation.

The most effective way of determining which approach is most likely to work for you is to go online and take a look at the range of methods employed by the recruitment industry. The quality of your CV is a major determinant of the progress you will make. Posting your CV on job boards will potentially give you access to a very wide range of potential employers and agencies, but only if you are able to adequately convey your skills and achievements. Increasingly CVs are scanned electronically for key words before any human intervention.

Search

At the senior end of the market, search firms continue to provide a key means of access to jobs. There are a number of reasons for this. In some cases confidentiality is the driver, with a need to identify potential successors for business leaders who are voluntarily or involuntarily about to depart. Opportunity costs are also a driver where a search firm, which really knows the market and the movers and shakers within it, is well placed to engage with and assess talent more effectively than the employer. A brand which is seeking to rebuild its reputation may also choose to use a search firm to "sell" the job to those potential candidates who may be wary, based on an outdated perception of the organisation's problems.

Search firms may advertise in support of their market trawl. They will certainly undertake a high level of research, some of which is desk based. So, once again, the quality of the collateral you have really matters – whether in the shape of a CV, conference presentations, your entries on professional networking sites or the positive perceptions of your peers and clients.

Just as recruitment agencies vary in quality, so do search firms. It is very naïve to believe that one search firm is the answer to your prayers. And do not assume that as a former client of a firm, they will be able to help you! Search firms have different relationships with various clients. Some have a strategic connection where they are well connected to the organisation and its strategy and ambitions. Others may have an opportunistic connection which may be based on a particular skill set or market know-how and may have won a mandate for this assignment with little prior knowledge of the organisation. Some firms are significantly more relationship oriented than others and consequently more likely to make time to meet someone on a speculative basis. Clearly if you know people at a particular firm, this is a good place to start. Alternatively ask people in your network to suggest – and recommend you – to a firm or firms.

In these instances or where you have been approached directly by a search firm for an exploratory discussion, it matters that as a potential candidate you recognise that you are "on show" throughout the entire process and that the quality of your CV is of major significance. Too often, very good candidates assume a poor CV will still get them an interview because "once they see me they will realise I can do this job". Unfortunately you are likely to suffer an early rejection. Remember you are not the only candidate and never ever underestimate the competition.

Neither should you overemphasise the power of an introduction. A search firm may have the highest regard for the person suggesting they should meet you; however, the firm does not know you and will need to satisfy themselves of your competence. So do some research on the firm and the people you are going to meet. A potential candidate who carries an attitude of entitlement is unlikely to persuade a search firm to go the extra mile to help them. Indeed a surprising number of potential candidates appear to feel the call from a search firm is, of itself, a mark of approval.

Be aware that however gentle the questioning at a first meeting, you **are** being assessed! Highly successful individuals who have risen to a senior level without too much effort can be particularly inward looking at this phase of the process with their "insight and outsight" buttons firmly in the "off" position.

The Director of a London search firm noted that: "I am always happy to see people from the market; it keeps me up to date and provides an opportunity to identify a potential candidate. I remain surprised at the number of senior people who do not appear to have done any due diligence before they meet us. This includes research on who we are and how we operate. This is often accompanied by an absence of thought on their next career step and the takeaway they wish to leave with us. Telling us how good they are without the evidence leaves an impression, albeit not a positive one. There are exceptions and that is when a senior person wants to take time out to review what may be the next step in a very successful career. An increasing number of people are doing this, seeking to test out what they really want."

So whether the conversation was initiated by you or the search firm, you must research the firm in question, just as you would a future employer:

- Who are the key people?

- Who are you meeting?

- What is their background?

- What clients and sectors does the firm specialise in?

- How much time will you have with them?

Just as we have identified the significance of understanding the importance of the **ROM** when looking at your current organisation or future employers, so should you identify the **ROM** expected from such a meeting:

- What do I want to get out of the meeting?

- What help are they able to give me?

- What impression do I want to leave?

- What will "success" look like?

The new CV

To move forward in any direction you do now need a CV. A focused three-pager building on all the effort you put into MBFCV. Unfortunately, simply cutting and pasting slabs of text from your MBFCV will not be sufficient. Writing a good CV isn't difficult but many people get frustrated in the process of creating something new and revert to using an old CV with a few updates, creating a document which will never be fit for purpose. Moreover it is all too easy to be inwardly focused on the task rather than focusing on the needs of the audience – so please put yourself in the shoes of potential readers. Without this perspective you may undersell your experience and achievements. Equally if you exaggerate your track record, this is going to become apparent at some point in the process.

It can be difficult to get the balance right, especially if you have worked in a collegiate environment, so draw on the work you did earlier and use the framework below to help you. Remember that despite the hours you may have spent crafting your CV, initially it may get a very cursory review so it's imperative to get key strengths across. Also bear in mind that it will most probably be viewed on screen so pay attention to formatting the "look" of the document both in print and electronically.

There are a variety of formats for presenting your CV and the template below will help you assemble the right information in a document that sells your expertise. Once you have a base CV it can be adjusted to suit the needs of each particular application and upon the feedback you will solicit. The internet has dramatically affected both our ability to produce a professional document and the ease with which it can be delivered. However, the need to sell you through a well-constructed CV remains a challenge. You need to produce a document which will grab the reader's attention without distracting them:

• Low on jargon

• High on positive and interesting sentences and easy to read

• Beware the gothic typeface!

• Concise

• No more than three pages – preferably two

• Accurate and specific

• Double check all dates

• Explain any gaps

My CV

Strapline/ what do I bring?	Your value statement – what differentiates me?
Dates	Accurate?
Accountabilities	Key objectives of each role
Demonstrable Competence Results Outcomes Solo/shared	Show what was delivered; if not with metrics, illustrate the outcomes. How were you able to engage with others and manage across boundaries?
Authenticity	See below
Contact Information	Accurate?
Update professional network information	Ensure consistency
Typos?	Double check! Do not rely on spell checker – read it! Getting the name of your employer wrong is a no-no (or maybe a know-know!), e.g. Procter & Gamble
Peer review	Get another view
Covering letter	See below

Strapline/what do I bring?

We are all encouraged to provide a short summary at the top of our CV to gain the attention of the reader and illustrate the "oomph" factor you will bring to a job. Many CVs fail to achieve this, merely summarising the text which follows. Reflect upon something like this:

WHAT DO I BRING?

Strategic and operational excellence

A senior professional with a track record of successfully transforming both balance sheets and mindsets, and delivering sustainable performance improvement and growth.

Crafting and communicating the vision

First-hand experience of confronting the need to develop innovative and robust approaches to significant market changes and to exploit opportunities before the competition. Able to build strong relationships with internal and external stakeholders to ensure success is not compromised.

A resilient and pragmatic approach

My own career journey has given me the opportunity to regularly review my own performance and to learn from experience.

This is merely an example; you must reflect upon how you can best differentiate yourself.

Authenticity

By itself a CV is useless if it does not reflect reality. It needs to be authentic and reflect the real you. To a reader, listener and observer, the way you describe yourself will make an impact in a variety of ways:

- **Language**. Is your career story plausible; are reverses explained; and are your responses to questions indicative of empathy with the needs of the role you would be moving into?

- **Patterns**. Frequent moves or no moves at all require explanation and context. Successively bigger roles in one organisation or regular moves based on being headhunted?

- **Cause and effect**. Did you move or were you pushed? What was the difference you personally made? You may feel you are currently working for the organisation from hell; expect to be questioned on what led you to move there in the first place and what this may signal about your judgement.

- **Trajectory.** Ever upward with no blips or a phased progression based on seeking appropriate opportunities? Have you reached your ceiling? Or are you someone who moves on "just in time"?

- **Understanding**. What are the lessons you have learned and the impact of this learning upon your approach to managing and leading? Learning from failure can be a key asset.

- **Rationale**. Why the interest in this role at this time?

- **The narrative/story**. Taken as a whole do you succeed in demonstrating your credibility as someone worthy of consideration for this or other roles? It could be that you trigger a thought on the part of the search firm about your suitability for assignments they are conducting for other clients.

The foregoing does not mean that you have carte blanche to airbrush away setbacks and failures. Many successful CEOs refer to unexpected failures as key moments in their development. So if things were difficult you need to be able to explain the circumstances and the outcomes.

For Board level appointments, authenticity is a window on an individual's integrity. How do they deal with corporate governance issues and reconcile the requirements of the market, regulator and their stakeholders. How compelling is their experience of effectively managing significant shocks to the brand and do they fully understand the significance of stress testing against tomorrow's challenges rather than yesterday's issues?

Ring ready or ring rusty?

The rationale for exploring authenticity at this point in the process is to ensure that you are alert to these issues before you have an initial conversation or first interview. To make yourself "ring ready" rather than remain "ring rusty" is the objective. Senior people with a strong track record can perform spectacularly badly during their first few interviews, having spent most of their career asking the questions rather than being challenged on motive and intent.

A case in point was an individual who had asked for some help in ensuring they made the best use of the time available during their forthcoming interview. The individual in question had substantial technical and business transformation experience and felt that this was not coming across in the interviews they had recently undertaken. Many senior managers require support to help them project their real impact in a manner which strikes an appropriate chord with the wide range of individuals involved in the hiring process. During role play a question was asked along the lines of: "Describe your experience of managing large-scale change and outline the seven key steps in the process." The answer which followed was lengthy – too lengthy. In part, the desire to identify the seven steps took over. In reality there could have been five or fifty; the need was for a response which showed a strategic and operational perspective on change. Interestingly this very topic came up at a "live" interview a few days later and a succinct answer was apparently forthcoming!

Support of this sort is not designed to help someone "fake" an interview performance but to enable the candidate to present themselves in an appropriate manner. Practice interviews can help a candidate baseline the effectiveness of their current approach and subsequently hone the ways in which they are able to genuinely "demonstrate competence". This support will not compensate for a lack of self-management skills and sometimes the lack of these leads to a misreading of what the purpose of the interview is. To reiterate it is both an opportunity and an assessment.

Collectively your responses will give your interviewers a sense of your cultural savvy and the degree to which you would be able to make the transition to a new role. This does not mean you should try to become a clone. For example, the reason many organisations have needed to transform themselves is an over-reliance on a restricted gene pool resulting in increasingly weak leadership teams. Renewal is significantly different to replication. In such circumstances both the candidate and the prospective employer will need to fully understand their collective and individual expectations. This can take time and needs to be underpinned by the search firm's sense of what their client may want and what the role may really require. A mismatch can lead to very embarrassing failures as evidenced by the recently promoted – and even more recently departed – Director General of the BBC who held the post for only two months.

Helping your recruitment agency or search firm to help you:

Stay focused. Do not assume that at your first meeting you will be asked the right questions to bring out the best of you, so take care to prepare thoroughly.

Build relationships. What goes around comes around. A strong relationship can benefit you in a number of ways over the longer term.

Practise transparency. Personal integrity matters and honesty will win out over hype.

Always remember the takeaway. What impression will remain after you have left the room; and what do you want to get out of the meeting?

Understand the process. Ask how the firm works and understand the typical stages of an assignment. Be aware that the process is, at its crudest, a great big filtering mechanism, so be clear on how the filters work.

You are the one with the need. They may be able to help you; in any event the more feedback you can get on your employability the better.

The job description

A significant issue in determining the focus of your CV, and indeed the interaction with recruiters or search firms, is how much you know about the vacancy. The point at which a job description is made available varies; for public sector roles it may be available on line as soon as the job is advertised, in other cases it may be made available after a preliminary discussion with potential candidates to determine whether they have the key skills required. Appendix A contains "Interview 101" which provides a reminder of key do's and don'ts. However experienced you perceive yourself to be, you must put yourself in the place of those who will interview you. Based on your experience and the role, what will they need to know about you, to place you on their shortlist? This may seem an obvious question to ask a candidate for a senior position, but seems to floor about a third of applicants: "If you get the job, what will you do during your first three months and what will success look like?"

Sometimes the competitive spirit can overtake realism. The job description is not designed to give you the opportunity to work out ways in which you can show how you might be able to perform or utilise skills that you have not yet mastered. This is the reason behind the use of the words "essential" and "desirable" in many job descriptions. You may well have the potential to master new skills which you do not currently possess and this may be of interest, although the organisation would no doubt have specified the role differently if this was what they really required at this time. Notwithstanding this, it is a good idea to seek clarity on this issue if you can. Sometimes the absence of a particular skill utilised in a specific setting is a deal breaker, e.g. a Six Sigma black belt with financial services experience. This can be very irritating for a candidate who has the skill but not the sector experience. However, whilst many skill sets and experience do "travel", the issue may be the timescale within which someone needs to get up to speed and assimilate other aspects of the role.

There will sometimes be an indication of the salary and benefits package. If this is way below your current package and below your "minimum", beware of thinking the organisation will be prepared to move upwards. Salary levels are generally easier to test out if you are dealing with a recruiter or search firm who will understand the logic underpinning the package – indeed they may have advised their client on what to offer. Sometimes jobs are over-specified and under-rewarded, particularly if there is a new round of cost reduction constraining pay levels. Important here is discovering the point at which your package will be reviewed if you do join the organisation and having commitment to such a review included in your contract.

The only true test of the reward package is the degree to which it attracts the right candidates for the right reasons. So simply applying for a role which is significantly smaller than your last post to get yourself back into employment may fail; you may be regarded as overqualified and potentially unable to adjust to a position which places you in a subordinate role. If you are applying for a job which is a "natural" next step but substantially better rewarded, you will need to be prepared to justify your worth and clearly demonstrate the scope and accountabilities of your current role.

Both overconfidence and a lack of commitment may come across in an interview without you consciously recognising this. Candidates who assume they must be a shoe-in for the role generally fail. Remember the organisation is going to go for the best fit with their needs. This does not mean that their needs may not shift in response to an outstanding candidate with a particular mix of skills and experience, but if you are unable to satisfy yourself that you tick all the "essential" boxes it may be much more fruitful to use your energies on opportunities that better match your career plan.

Non-Executive Directorships (NEDs)

In the not too distant past, NED roles came along through one's network. Thankfully these days "know-how" supported by "know-who" is essential. These roles are not appropriate for everyone and a recently appointed NED has reflected on their experience of the process and when an NED role is or is not an appropriate next step.

Why undertake an NED role?

Undertaking an NED role can provide a number of development opportunities at a variety of career stages, for example:

• As a career reaches its point of maturity such a role, or a portfolio of roles, can provide an opportunity to share experience and to transition towards retirement.

• In mid-career, an NED role can be an excellent vehicle for broadening experience and preparation for an executive director role.

• For a functional leader of an organisation, taking up an NED role can provide a freshening of ideas and an ability to compare and contrast practice in another business.

However, anyone considering using an NED role for development must fully consider the differences between non-executive and executive roles and whether their personality and style are suited to this. The role of the Board and the NEDs is to protect the interests of the shareholders and provide governance and independent challenge to the executive directors. To be effective, an NED needs to be able to provide feedback in a constructive and

---

supportive manner. It is essential that an NED recognises that their role is not to manage and direct the company. This reliance on influencing and coaching skills may require a significant shift in style for some senior leaders to succeed as an NED.

Preparing for and securing an NED role

A good way of helping an individual decide whether they are suited to an NED role is to undertake some form of NED training. A number of executive search companies run events which will often give opportunities to network with current NEDs and this will allow individuals to learn more about the skills and experience required from others. Some of the larger executive search firms provide from half-day to full-day training events, often providing learning on the NED role by undertaking role playing of Board meetings. Although such programmes are recognised as excellent, the events tend to be annual and the cost of attending can be high.

Due to the focus over the last couple of years on increasing the ratio of women on UK Boards, a number of training events aimed at encouraging women to seek Board roles have been developed. A number of these programmes, run by both executive search and professional services firms, are of high quality. Most of these programmes are composed of a series of two-hour sessions covering a variety of topics relating to non-executive roles. Some of these programmes also provide coaching to individuals from current NEDs and some will provide networking opportunities with the chairmen and staff from the Board practices of key executive search firms.

Attending such a programme can not only provide individuals with a comprehensive view of the NED role but also help them to decide if they are suited to such a role and provide them with contacts to secure a position.

Ten years ago, many NED roles were filled by networking and contacts with chairmen, without the help of search firms. However, most NED roles are currently filled by commissioned search firms. Most of the larger search firms have consultants that specialise in non-executive Board recruitment. There are also some niche companies that specialise in this area. Public sector NED roles are normally advertised so you need to scan the press and register on appropriate government websites.

It is essential that if you are interested in attaining an NED role, you should:

• Clearly analyse which parts of your experience would be useful for a Board role.

• Develop a CV of no more than two pages which outlines the key elements of your experience which could be utilised by a Board and make the search firm's job easy!

• Ensure that the right area of the search firm is contacted, being known on the executive side of the firm is no guarantee that a person will be in the frame for NED roles.

• Ensure you have a full, clear briefing from the recruiter on the people being met and any particular idiosyncrasies.

- Prepare well for meetings, read the Annual Report, ask the recruiter for analyst reports, look at the website and list questions.

- Be prepared for a lot of meetings – you may meet all members of the Board separately prior to appointment.

- Gain feedback from the recruiter.

- Preserve your network. Don't be afraid to use your own network and follow up on leads.

The recruitment and selection timescale

Finding the right candidate can take some time. Whilst your application may be the most important thing on your horizon at the present time, organisations usually have many other priorities. Moreover, do not place undue reliance on a particular application being successful. You need to maintain your level of focus and activity until you have accepted an offer and have a signed contract. It could well be that the offer you get is not in line with your expectations or promises made, so maintain your focus and momentum and do not ease up.

Below is a very simplified iteration of the steps in the process:

- The organisation identifies a need. Depending on the seniority of the role this may lead to:

  - An internal move

  - Advertising in the national, local or trade press

  - Posting the job on the appropriate job boards

  - Asking a variety of recruitment agencies if they can help

- Briefing a search firm

- This may, or may not lead to further action:

  - The individual whose departure created the need decides to stay

  - Cost control measures lead to the post being merged with other existing jobs

  - Coincidentally a CV arrives from a suitably qualified candidate who is interviewed and subsequently gets the job

  - Coincidentally a speculative CV arrives from a suitably qualified candidate who is referred to the recruiter/search firm

- The external recruiter/search firm is given the assignment and use a variety of methods to identify candidates:

  - Research including trawling sites such as LinkedIn and conversations with connections in the particular sector/market

  - Word-of-mouth recommendations

  - Telephone discussions with potential candidates

  - CVs requested from those who appear to be best suited

  - Job description made available

  - Telephone interviews

  - Face-to-face interview(s)

  - Shortlist of preferred candidates presented to employer

- Employer interviews and assesses selected candidates along with any internal candidates.

- A decision is made; an offer is made. If the offer is accepted, references will be taken up. If not, other shortlisted candidates may be contacted. Unsuccessful candidates will be informed.

As anyone who has dealt with recruiters or search firms will know, there are many points at which delays can occur and in this era of cost control a recruitment process begun in good faith could be curtailed in the early stages. The public sector is an exception, with clear deadlines for the submission of an application and early notice of the dates of interviews. The public sector is also likely to require a competence-based application form to be completed. This will be the core driver of shortlisting so you need to give your full attention to providing the information requested.

The number of people involved in the process, the number of interviews and the assessment methods used all potentially lengthen the duration of the process. Whatever the stage and however important the outcome is to you, remember that the organisation and its advisers will have many other issues on their agenda. Very frequent calls asking for an update will get you remembered for the wrong reasons.

Some professional service firms are known for extremely lengthy selection processes and the same rule applies: keep focused on your job search until you have an offer or offers. The upside is that this may be because you are being given the opportunity to meet a number of potential colleagues – not in a formal interview context but to give you a better insight into the organisation. However, sometimes the process may be particularly chaotic. There may be good reasons for this but this may indeed be the way in which the organisation behaves on a daily basis.

Saying "no"

Rejecting an offer that on reflection does not seem to match your needs or expectations needs careful consideration. There may be a number of reasons for this:

- A counter-offer from your existing employer. This is by no means rare but there are two issues to be aware of. Many people have disengaged more than they realise and a late counter-offer may only provide limited motivation to remain with the organisation for any length of time. Moreover, revisit your **ROM** criteria to confirm the validity of your decision.

- Despite your due diligence and a package that meets your expectations, you are not sure this is the right organisation for you. Underlying this could be a failure on the part of the employer to understand that the organisation they fondly describe to candidates is a work in progress rather than the finished object. This may not be deliberate; rather the desire to get the "right" person for the future has been embraced with too much enthusiasm. For a transformation expert who gets bored by a steady state business, this may be their ideal role. However, for someone expecting to grow the business rather than restructure it this may be the job of their nightmares.

- An "offer" from another employer that has revived a search. The issue here is whether this is actually an offer or an expression of renewed interest. Will you need to go through the process again? Unfortunately a book cannot answer this dilemma. We sometimes hear what we want to hear; you may simply be asked if you are still interested in being a candidate once the search resumes.

Without having the power to move from one parallel universe to the other it is difficult to know if you have made the right choice until some time has elapsed. Revisiting the criteria underpinning your career choices and discussing your dilemma with people you trust will help – as will an honest, open discussion with your search firm.

The supporting letter

In this era of text messages, letter writing is an increasing rarity. However a short, focused letter can gain the reader's attention if it succinctly outlines why you are applying. This is not the opportunity to repeat verbatim what is in your CV. Do your research on the organisation and re-read the job description or advert and meld your rationale to their needs covering:

- What you bring – your track record

- How you fit the organisation's needs - your capacity and capability and why the organisation is attractive to you

- When you will follow up with a phone call

This need be no more than three short paragraphs. It is designed to get the recipient to read your CV and is not a substitute for it. If you say you will call to follow up on progress be sure to do so!

Getting help

A good outplacement provider will provide support and practice in all aspects of the recruitment and selection process, and some search firms and recruitment agencies may be able to give you additional ideas on the opportunities upon which you should be focusing. They should also be prepared to give you feedback on your interviews with the organisation, should you get to that stage. If you want some feedback on psychometric tests, ask for it. A perennial difficulty is the degree to which this feedback is as full as it might be. It may be that the organisation has reasons for a rejection which they prefer to keep to themselves.

The Takeaway

Many people fall into the trap of feeling they have discovered their ideal next job and are sure they will be hired. You must keep exploring until you have accepted an offer, so don't ease up too soon!

Chapter Nine
Arriving and Delivering

"A career is a series of ups and downs, of comebacks."

Steve Guttenberg

The plethora of books on "the first hundred days" shows this phase of the career journey can sometimes be problematic. The characteristics of the effective self-manager need to kick in here. I once gave a talk on the first hundred days and used the theme of "lost in space" as a metaphor to illustrate how "landing" on a new organisation might feel akin to arriving on an alien landscape where:

- The atmosphere is somehow different

- Decision-making seems almost gravity defying

- Finding the horizon is difficult, as is looking over it

- The language is different and outsiders need to fend for themselves

This may be somewhat exaggerated, but it is impossible to overstate the importance of the first few months – especially in the case of senior appointments.

More generally, moving into a new job represents both an opportunity and a challenge. This is not always appreciated by your new colleagues who know their way around the organisation and, unless they have joined recently, may assume that if you need to know anything you will ask! It is surprisingly common for someone to be asked to produce their own object-ives, which does provide an opportunity – if taken – to work with your boss on fleshing out your new role.

Paradoxically it seems that, on occasion, contractors and interim workers get a more thorough introduction than a new full-timer; whether this is to ensure these individuals deliver from day one has never been terribly clear. There will fre-quently be an induction process to ensure you do get to meet people and receive an introduction to the organisation encom-passing everything from values to products to IT systems. Many of these programmes are delivered, at least in part, online. If such a programme is not available the best bet is to speak to your boss and HR to create a schedule of meetings that will give you an appropriate understanding of the people and functions you will be working with day to day.

For more senior hires, the first hundred days are the time to take stock of the organisation from the perspective of the leader of the team, function or company and to ensure understanding of the new role and its boundaries. Meeting the challenge of hitting the ground running, making an impact and securing early wins is initially as much about understanding as taking immediate action.

However, progressing from arrival to delivery mode is, after all, what you are there for. Sometimes an individual may be undone by mistaking coping strategies for a genuine strategic perspective. This is well illustrated by the examples below provided by Matthew K McCreight, Managing Partner at Schaffer Consulting, who differentiates between "planning" and "achieving":

The Planner

This new CEO focused on strategy and leadership:

Prior to starting new role, kept a low profile. Did not want to "ruffle any feathers", especially of the outgoing CEO.

Spent the first six months getting oriented to the company and developing a high-level strategy to drive growth.

Then took the next six months to reorganise his leadership team, having them carry out detailed implementation planning.

Within the first few months of his second year in role, rolled out the new strategy across the organisation.

After 24 months, the company's revenues were largely unchanged.

The Achiever

This new CEO focused on strategy, leadership and results:

Used several months prior to starting the new job to shape and test their vision and aspirations.

Prepared plans to "get out of the starting blocks" quickly.

Convened management team one month into new role to agree on: 1) a stretch, 2) a one-year stretch revenue goal, and 3) areas for moving into action within the first three months. Some areas focused on improving basic results – sales, service, and efficiency. Others focused on sharpening strategic direction and building management capabilities.

> *Built leadership priorities and processes around the strategic goals and sponsored other rapid results-oriented efforts along the way to get the organisation moving and achieving.*
>
> *Convened the leadership team four times in the next 12 months to keep building their leadership, sharpening their shared strategy and increasing momentum on goals for better performance.*
>
> After first year, revenues increased by 25%.

Of significance is the contrast between the "don't ruffle feathers" approach and the "get out of the starting blocks quickly" mode of assimilation.

Superior performers might have been expected to exhibit the achievement-oriented characteristics as their career has developed. In part this will depend on where – and, importantly, for whom – they have worked along with their own leadership competencies. The scale of the challenge may only become apparent upon joining although given the nature of the economic challenges facing organisations, the repertoire required for success needs to be thoroughly assessed during the hiring process. What demonstrable competence does the individual exhibit in:

- Identifying key issues and challenges and crafting strategic options and tasks

- Creating high-level, organisation-specific scenarios

- Developing deliverables able to be implemented quickly

- Building a long-term signposted route to success

- Planning delivery and organising execution

- Tackling change in the organisation

- Tracking progress

It may be that the employing organisation has drastically underestimated what is really needed to reposition the organisation, so the importance of due diligence on the part of the candidate is crucial. Misperception on the part of the new employer is not your ally!

For insiders such as returning international assignees and internal promotees there may also be unexpected challenges. There can be even more when an individual gains a bigger role by virtue of a "hostile" acquisition. In this instance you aren't in your "old" environment; you're potentially isolated in what may feel like "enemy" territory. In these circumstances the themes explored in the chapter on mapping are very relevant since you will need to assess your level of comfort with the organisation you now find yourself part of, without having had the opportunity to reflect on the attractions of working for your new employer during the recruitment and selection process.

One's understanding of culture, boundary and role issues is never absolutely clear until you are on the inside and it is important to connect with the organisation to create new working relationships and use both your insight and outsight to understand the formal and informal workings of the organisation. In so doing, take your own preferences into account – your preferred ways of working may not mesh precisely with the organisation you have joined. Working out what is really expected of you can be more complex than anticipated; are your expectations and those of your key stakeholders mutually compatible?

Executive coaching

It is for these reasons that the role of executive coaching during this phase of employment is so frequently discussed. Working with an executive coach during this period can significantly accelerate the speed with which a new incumbent assimilates the ways in which the organisation works, and identifies opportunities for maximising their contribution to the strategic needs of the business. For most senior managers this is a time of adjustment as well as action, and having the time and space for reflection on what's really required with an external sparring partner potentially supports focus and direction. Depending on the seniority of the role, there is also a benefit for the participant's boss/chairman in the form of an agreed and open process to support their own management of, and support for, a new colleague. This is sometimes provided as part of the assimilation phase in a new role by the search firm; more frequently it is purchased separately. A number of CEOs have commented that the provision of a coach was something they negotiated as part of their package. In other words, they sought it rather than were offered it. Indeed, some have paid for the coach themselves.

At a time when delivering rather than assimilating is in the ascendancy, the value of this support is still questioned. In some cases the organisation feels it is able to provide the support internally, in others the belief is that the search process is robust enough to have delivered a candidate who, for the present, will not require this type of support.

These are the observations of two people who did use executive coaching when moving into a new role:

FIRST PERSON

"What I thought I needed was the classic sparring partner to test out my ideas on strategy. I had some grandiose plans for shifting the direction of the business. As things turned out, I was unprepared for the difference between my management style and that of my new CEO. I was able to work through my likely – and indeed actual – reactions to challenge and pressure. I hadn't realised how averse I can be to what in my eyes is "conflict". My coach helped me adopt a proactive approach to managing my boss which involved working through his likely reactions and developing strategies to handle them. Although I had done a number of psychometric tests at various points in my career, this was the first time I had the opportunity to think – and feel – what they really meant to me."

SECOND PERSON

"The opportunity to describe what has been happening and reflect upon things with an outsider has given me a greater insight than I would have gained left to my own devices. Working harder is not the same as working smarter and I have gained new insights into my response when plans get disrupted. It has also been very useful to explore my feelings about the way the organisation makes decisions."

Whether or not executive coaching is utilised, it is important for the executive to take the time to understand their new environment and the expectations of their new employer. Without understanding, action is likely to be counterproductive. At this time a coach can significantly help a newcomer by providing a regular opportunity during the first few months to act as a sounding board for their observations and feelings about the way the organisation appears to behave.

Interestingly, although many new hires feel themselves to be reasonably clear about these issues, those who have used a coach in the past are more likely to use one now. The new employer may not see coaching as an important need; in part because of their own due diligence on the successful candidate and also because they have commissioned a robust search and assessment process to identify an individual able to cope with both the organisation as it is now, and also have the capacity and capability to guide it through uncharted waters should the need arise.

That said, just as financial institutions are required to stress test their financial strength, for top jobs there is a very strong argument for something similar for candidates. This is particularly important in the case of very strong technical candidates who may need to contend with a systemic shock such as a major PR or brand crisis as the leader of the organisation. Recent examples include the BBC and BP. These events do occur with some regularity, such as the recent cases of an allegedly contaminated dairy product in the Chinese market and an uncontrollable underground fire in a UK colliery.

The **ROM** agenda you set yourself should include:

- Time to reflect on the organisation and to take stock of one's own feelings about the future. This is going to allow you to benchmark the organisation against your expectations and baseline the start point from which changes may appear necessary.

- Managing upwards is a critical skill. There are new stakeholders (Chairman, Board, CEO) to build relationships with.

- Managing outwards: position yourself to be able to proactively deal with analysts, regulators, the media and trade unions and others from an early stage.

- Building the new team which will require a dispassionate assessment of your "inheritance" and the resources required for the future.

- Strategic networking both within and outside the organisation. Professor David Sims, formerly of Cass Business School, has commented that "the really effective leaders are the ones who know what to lean on other people for...they make sure they have a good network of people."

- Active two-way communication to both "mark your territory" and ensure your antennae are fully deployed to understand the culture of the organisation and a first view of fitness for purpose. The sooner you begin to walk the job, the sooner you will be able to move from assimilation to delivery.

- Considering one's own feelings about the move and understanding how these feelings show up to others.

- Managing one's career in the new organisation will require you to periodically remind yourself of the need to deploy all the facets of effective self-management; people are often good at doing their jobs but surprisingly bad at selling themselves inside their organisation.

Some of these topics will require more consideration if they emerge as concerns which are down to a mismatch between due diligence before appointment and the post-employment awareness. This may be an intuitive sense that things may not be as they seem or promises made not being fulfilled. The latter may revolve around the clarity of roles and boundaries. Concerns over reporting lines, membership of key committees and apparent blurring of accountabilities arise more often than the reader might expect.

For any senior role you would expect that there will have been full discussion during the selection process on what the key aspects and deliverables of the job are; this is by no means universal. Occasionally there may have been a change of personnel and the individual to whom you were to report has left or moved within the organisation. Sometimes what is promised at the interview does not materialise; the job is as "sold" along with the job title but not the reporting line. Internal turf wars can also restrict the scope of a newcomer as individuals move to protect their own "territory". Equally, the emergence of new functional areas such as that of Chief Risk Officer in the insurance industry and the reshaping of compliance in the financial services industry will require a period of time to bed down and in so doing will lead to a broader reshaping of functional responsibilities.

The Takeaway

For the candidate, the message is as before – take the need to do your own due diligence seriously and meet as many people as you can from your new organisation. Sometimes this is only feasible once an appointment is announced; in any event, if your assimilation has been effective you will have acquired the knowledge, awareness and stimulus to determine both the agenda for future action and the means to execute the delivery.

Chapter Ten
Consolidating and Reviewing

"A man wrapped in himself makes a very small bundle."

Benjamin Franklin

The brevity of this chapter should not disguise its significance. Effective career management is a continuous process:

Focus on delivery. Just as you should be managing your own career trajectory, so should you focus on the needs of your team and of the organisation. The reputation people build does precede them, not just within the organisation but outside it.

Maintain your channels of communication and understand the approach your boss prefers for being briefed. Most of us do not like surprises; if you feel you do not get enough airtime with the people you need to, ensure that you are, nonetheless, keeping them in the picture.

Keep networking. Managing within complex organisations and, indeed, smaller units needing a turnaround can consume huge amounts of energy, both physical and emotional. Most of the resources will probably be directed inwards. So whilst an internal network is a prerequisite, don't lose touch with your external networks. These may be professional and technical, social and academic.

Scan the horizon. In part, this is a consequence of remaining well connected through your networking. It is also about future positioning – testing out and keeping up to date with "what if" scenarios to look forward to see how the organisation, market and your own role may evolve. This helps you to identify which elements of your experience and competency set are likely to be relevant in tomorrow's environment and also where there are gaps or development needs which will impact upon your employability.

Ensure you seek and are open to receiving timely feedback. Create your own timescale for proactively seeking feedback from your boss, colleagues and customers and stick to it. Just be aware of feedback fatigue!

Regularly update your ROM and career plan. This will enable you to benchmark whether you are where you want to be at this point in your career. Maybe your ambitions and expectations will have shifted. This does not imply dissatisfaction; you may have found a great job in a great organisation! It is also useful to take stock to enable you to make a meaningful comparison between your job and others that you sometimes hanker after. Having taken a look at what's on offer elsewhere and researched the market, you may discover there is more upside in your current organisation. Ambitions and goals do change over time so you may also discover that you are no longer driven to gain successively larger roles.

That said, if you are uncertain and do not seem to be getting the traction you expected, a simple diagnostic is to take a sheet of A4 paper and draw a picture of your job and how it interfaces with the rest of the organisation. This is likely to include membership of committees, working parties and projects as well as the key channels through which your deliverables are conveyed. This is not a test of your artistic temperament and will often take a little longer than anticipated as you get into the detail of mapping the complexities of your role. You can take a look at this for yourself and reflect on underlying issues that may be "interfering" with your job. Even better is to talk through the picture with someone you trust. Frequently boundary, accountability and role definition issues become clearer as you take a third party through your sense of what your picture is describing. This provides a means of putting barriers and opportunities into perspective and, as you articulate what's going on, ways of resolving some of these challenges may become clearer.

Chapter Eleven
The Organisational Imperative – Why Supporting Career Management Matters

"It is wise to keep in mind that neither success nor failure is ever final."

Roger Babson

This chapter provides an overview of some of the issues confronting organisations as they work to attract, retain and develop their people. Recognising the talent you already have is discussed in the context of organisational change as is the challenge of building new skills in response to regulatory and market changes. It concludes with an exploration of how the concept of **ROM** can build bridges between employee engagement, talent development and performance management.

Global downturn or not, depending on location or sector the "war for talent" holds good in some cases whilst in others the "war on talent" is perceived to be pervasive. The organisational counterweight to career management is talent management. Identifying the high-potential people needed to fulfil near and longer-term goals is clearly a strategic need. In practice, the policies and procedures to not only identify but also to attract, develop, engage and retain these individuals will vary. The scale and scope of such approaches ranges from sophisticated global rotation planning within multinationals to simpler succession planning in smaller organisations. The population targeted will range from new graduates, cohorts of specialists and next generation leaders.

The Annual Survey Report 2013, on Resourcing and Talent Planning from CIPD and Hays notes that "despite relatively high unemployment numbers, employers in a number of sectors are struggling to find enough skilled and experienced individuals to fill the posts available". The report also notes that some organisations are adapting their recruitment methods to become more accessible to younger candidates and working hard to understand the role of social media and focusing on succession planning. "The findings highlight the importance of building a powerful employer brand that will resonate with current and future employees."

Whilst some organisations may be struggling to attract and retain talent this is by no means universal. Indeed it would be foolhardy for any reader wanting to take personal ownership of their career to make assumptions about what their employer may or may not be planning for the organisation – and for them!

A risk is always going to be an obsession with metrics rather than cause and effect. Organisations may commit acts of "metrocity" where a survey result or KPI (Key Performance Indicator) is seen as an end in itself. The challenge is to use measures which support subsequent analysis, review and action.

Measurement – the aggregate return on investment

Developing meaningful measures for reviewing not only value for money but consistently exceeding performance expectations:

- Labour turnover: voluntary versus involuntary?

- Internal promotion versus external hires?

- Where will our next generation leaders come from?

- Why are we unable to hire the people we want?

- What is the potential cost/loss to the organisation of not investing?

Improvement – the organisation's return on people:

- What do we need to do to fully engage our people?

- What do we need to do to ensure retention of key talent and achievement of potential?

- How effective are our processes for developing the talent of the future?

Engagement – the individual's "Return on Me"

Developing a framework which enables your people to:

- Better understand themselves and their aspirations

- Identify potential career options within the organisation

- Understand and initiate an adult dialogue with the organisation

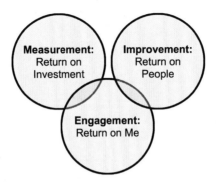

The Return on Investment and Return on People measures probably show up in some form in most organisations. They are effectively the questions the organisation and managers will use to examine the return they are getting from their workforce and form the basis of discussions on "the return we (the organisation) expect from you (the employee)". Less common is a process to provide the employee with the opportunity to discuss the returns they expect from their job and the organisation. The role of the **ROM** in achieving this is explored below.

There are implications for both individuals and organisations in these measures. For example, an organisation under financial pressure and market competition is likely to focus on the value derived from learning and development. The short-term view may prevail with budgets cut and programmes curtailed. In these circumstances, the challenge for the individual may well be how best to make a plausible case for getting their employer to meet their development needs. The corollary will be the HR function attempting to make the case for retaining their budget to ensure key talent is retained.

Talent management

The good news is that many organisations have maintained their commitment to talent management during the downturn and as new opportunities, technologies and markets emerge, are adapting their approach to ensure they are able to source the talent they anticipate requiring in the future. An interesting example is the Tunnel and Underground Construction Academy which has been established to support the £14.5 billion Crossrail project and develop the key skills required to work in tunnel excavation and underground construction. The impetus came from the 3,500 jobs required to deliver the programme and to ensure a lasting legacy of skills to support the UK construction industry. The scale of the project will also ensure that the skills acquired will be attractive across construction projects worldwide.

In the nuclear sector, the UK Government Nuclear Research and Development Advisory Board published a paper on "Meeting UK Nuclear Skills Needs to 2050 – A Unified Strategy for World-Class R&D Skills Development". This set out a number of recommendations to support the regeneration of the UK's high-level nuclear R&D skills base and referred to a future skills strategy which might also include: "The strategic planning of career pathways for talented individuals, coupled with creative ways of retaining Subject Matter Experts in the nuclear sector beyond formal retirement. This would allow individuals to develop the technical and other skills needed to excel in their specialist field, contribute over a longer timeframe, and also impart their knowledge to others." (Nuclear Energy SKills Alliance, Annual review, 2013.)

Of itself talent management can deliver little unless it is embedded in the organisation, aligned to business strategy and included in the business planning process. If not, the risk is that skills required in the future are not anticipated and the development needs of next generation leaders may go unnoticed. Equally, time and focus may be diverted to superficially attractive but ultimately unproductive initiatives. Without this connectivity the talent machine can become a behemoth with a life of its own.

In any organisation there will always be tensions between organisational needs and individual expectations. Talent management does not always sit in the HR function; in larger organisations it may be separated. If so, the need to ensure a joined-up understanding of all people processes at operational and strategic levels must be mandated. Without this convergence a variety of consequences may follow with "talent management" perceived as a corporate centre/head office issue with a wide range of inclusion and exclusion issues sure to follow.

The deliverables expected from employee engagement may also become blurred, with "vicarious" employee engagement rather than active employee engagement coming out the winner, at least in the short term. The more visible the support of senior managers as sponsors of talent management initiatives, the more likely they are to be effective. However, the day-to-day managers of those embraced by talent management initiatives also need support and direction to enhance their role as key players in the process. It is here that talent management may show up as being "done to" a chosen few, which has implications for the transparency of the process and the strength of working relationships across the organisation.

At the most basic level, organisations need to have clarity over:

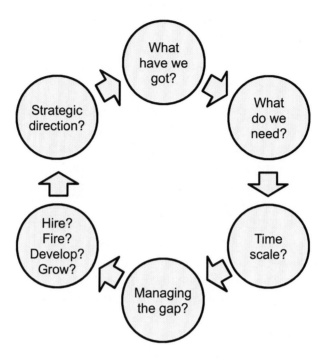

Whilst this may look remarkably simple on paper, making it work in practice is no pushover. There are many ways of assessing success including:

- Outputs which are relevant for the organisation and include turnover/retention and impact of those included in talent management programmes

- Outcomes which are clearly related to outputs but may have a more qualitative element to them, e.g. the proportion of home-grown talent in senior management positions over a rolling three-year period. Are development programmes talked about with enthusiasm by participants and viewed as valuable by the rest of the organisation?

- Stickability. Does the programme produce a discernible – and measurable – long-term difference to both the organisation and participants?

Whatever the measures, the data underpinning them may cause disagreement at the highest levels. In August 2013, The Royal College of Midwives issued a statement suggesting that the gap between the numbers of midwives the NHS in England currently employs and the number required will not be closed until 2026: "England remains around 5,000 midwives short of the number required to provide mothers and babies with the high-quality service they need and deserve." This view was countered by the Government Minister accountable for maternity services, arguing that the figures fail to take account of the 5,000 trainee midwives who will qualify in the next three years. These comments serve to illustrate that anticipated skill and talent shortages will always be an inexact science.

In the UK it has been suggested that the decline of defined benefit pension schemes would ultimately lead to a reduction in both activity and job opportunities. However, in July 2013 the Pensions Management Institute suggested (Press release 2013) that: "Industry predictions around defined benefit legacy issues, especially involving buy-out, being completed within 25-30 years are wildly over-optimistic, with the reality much closer to 50 years." Clearly a range of other factors may emerge during this lengthy interval but its forecast does serve to show the importance of looking over the horizon and having robust processes in place to cope with anticipated, and unexpected, supply and demand issues.

Whenever new industries, markets or technologies emerge there can be a scramble for talent because the speed of the change may lead to tactical rather than strategic responses. As a clearer understanding of what is really required emerges, this is often accompanied by an awareness that the bench strength required to tackle these needs has either been underestimated or yet to be developed. The very nature of markets will also ensure that, at about the same time, most of your competitors will also realise that there is a market shortage of the individuals with the requisite skills!

As was the case with information technology some decades ago, an understanding of what is really required combined with a shortage of individuals with the necessary competence can lead to knee-jerk responses rather than considered action. In fairness this is an easy judgement to make with hindsight whereas at the time the actual range of options may be limited. However, patterns of behaviour do have a habit of repeating themselves over time and include:

- Mitigation of the immediate "problem" by moving individuals into new roles, for which they may not have been fully prepared. The needs of other teams or functions may be compromised as individuals are redeployed and succession plans disrupted. This is not all bad news since most of us at some point in our careers will have been fortunate enough to get a "lucky break". However, being dragooned into a role with little interest at very short notice also has the capacity to disengage people.

- Substitution through the use of external consultants to support short-term needs, which may lead to delays in developing a structured approach to "growing your own talent". A particular challenge created by substitution is ensuring there is an effective process by which the consultants' know-how is transferred and embedded into the organisation. Without this, a "black box" mentality may emerge with an inadequate understanding of what has been done and longer-term dependency on expensive external expertise.

- Interim hiring of contractors on short-term contracts who may, if successful, turn out to be a permanent solution. However, unless appropriately supervised, interims cause significant problems if their expertise is not at the level required. The combination of an interim who has apparently "done this work many times before" allied to in-house inexperience and uncertainty may result in a halo effect which can be very damaging. This is a particular risk in any field where skills are scarce, since track records and reputations may be difficult to benchmark. There will also be many examples where an interim role fits both the individual's career objectives and competencies and the organisation's needs very well.

- Imitating a competitor's approach and/or poaching their people. Poaching from competitors may well deliver new hires of appropriate quality but may also drive up salary levels, which in turn creates a new set of challenges for the organisation and the labour market as a whole. Organisations may – rarely – revert to an approach genuinely resembling panic when a view takes hold that they must acquire X and Y before the competition hires them.

- Underestimating what is really required, placing unreasonable demands on a newly promoted or externally hired "expert".

It may be that short-term help will provide the support to cope with immediate issues allowing the company the space to draw up a hiring plan, but an integrated approach is a necessity if appropriately targeted hiring and development are to be successful:

- What do we really want from this role or function, and who can help us work this out?

- What are the key enablers and barriers to success?

- What is our current bench strength; what talent do we have that could be fast-tracked?

- What roles do we need to fill now and are we able to adequately describe roles, boundaries, accountabilities and future career direction?

A recent case in point is the emergence of the risk function in the insurance industry. In part, this has assumed greater significance by virtue of the need to comply with the requirements of the Solvency II Directive which has implications for capital requirements, governance and disclosure processes. The challenge has been exacerbated by the ambiguity surrounding the date at which the Directive will come into force. For some organisations, this requirement significantly challenged the assumptions underpinning both their medium-term talent pipeline and their short-term talent needs.

The challenge for the insurance industry has been the shortage of individuals who are rounded and grounded with the competencies to deliver what is required, both technically and as a functional leader. In some cases, the default of appointing individuals who are technically excellent but unproven in roles which require the post holder to robustly challenge NEDs has been found wanting. In others, an individual who got a "lucky break" will have been given – and taken – the opportunity to flourish. There are also implications in the changing risk environment for those overseeing the function. Executives and non-executives are coming to terms with the need to look beyond risk models and the assumptions upon which they are predicated.

The views of senior people in the insurance sector exemplify concern about ambiguity and the need for longer-term perspectives:

- "All I hear is Solvency II; it's important but the role of CRO goes far wider than mere compliance."

- "As the regulatory regime has been perceived as more important, we've probably over-promoted people without the capability to take our approach to the next level."

- "We've boosted the function with more and more consultants – however, body shopping is not the answer."

- "We need people who understand risk and can authoritatively convey their concerns to the Board."

The role of the Chief Risk Officer is particularly interesting in this regard. An effective Chief Risk Officer will need a combination of:

- Technical strength

- Environmental savvy; proactive individuals who understand the complexities of the risk environment

- Self-aware and alert to how they may respond when under pressure

- Team players able to influence and energise the organisation's approach to risk

These are not characteristics that are currently found in great abundance in the insurance sector and consequently will require some innovative thinking on how best to identify and assess candidates and also how to shape internal development programmes.

Leaving aside the twists and turns of Solvency II, the processes used to develop talent in a "business as usual" environment typically include a variety of succession plans which will be supported at various levels in the organisation. They should be focused on learning and development programmes and underpinned by planned job rotations, secondments, international assignments, and membership of project teams. There may be functional or global talent pools focusing on specific needs such as engineers or linguists. An emerging trend, building on the experience of in-company MBAs, is the evolution of the corporate university.

The key issues underpinning success are all linked to the "line of sight" ranging from the visibility of the CEO as the organisation's Chief Talent Officer to the need to be able to assess the difference talent initiatives make to the individual and to the organisation. Whilst big-ticket, high-profile programmes may be seductive, do they really deliver skills transferrable to the workplace and enhance organisational performance? Are more focused approaches preferable that are targeted at specific needs?

Transparency: A clear and openly communicated statement of purpose, the criteria for being considered as a potential participant in any initiative and the application/referral process are necessary. In some organisations, access is determined by line managers at unit level; in others, global programmes may have some form of assessment as the prerequisite to attendance. Inclusion and exclusion have the potential to send mixed messages to participants and non-participants alike and the strategic concern must be to ensure all avenues available to develop the workforce are exploited and the goals underpinning them clearly communicated.

Managing expectations: Entry to a particular scheme being seen as a "gift" can be countered by ensuring that participants understand their personal accountability for learning and performing. This will be reinforced by having the appropriate processes in place to test out potential participants' expectations and exploring their ideas and personal goals. It also needs to be understood that membership of a talent pool is subject to review and that inclusion is not a "guarantee" of career progression.

This is particularly relevant in the context of increasing diversity. Lord Davies commented in the second annual review of "Women on Boards" (April 2013) that: "The executive pipeline is not an easy nut to crack. On the outside it sounds quite simple; organisations need to attract the best people at the start of their careers, spot and nurture their talent and ensure that they have good development routes, offering challenges, variety, role models, mentoring and career progression in a supportive environment. Succession plans help to ensure that senior management pools are well developed and that the company is well equipped to handle any unforeseen events. Of course this takes time and we could not expect to see well-developed pipelines overnight. Nevertheless, companies really need to think about what they are doing to develop talent across their organisations to ensure that they are well equipped for the future."

Assessment: For both the individuals and the organisation it is important that participants' involvement is supplemented by regular reviews and feedback. Without this, the notion of "success" can be viewed simply as membership of a particular scheme or attendance at a particular series of workshops, rather than the demonstrable value of the learning and experience gained in accelerating career progression and enhancing organisational performance.

Support: More focused interventions may prove useful in the shape of coaching and mentoring as preparation for bigger roles or for high-potential individuals deemed at risk of derailment. There are a number of factors that lead to derailment. The key issue is working with individuals to give them the awareness of what their default may be under duress or the implications of an overused strength. Frustration may be another issue. As a management consultant, I was sometimes alerted by a client to someone who was "difficult". Generally these were able people who found their current role unfulfilling or presented their views with a vigour that their managers found very challenging. So although an organisation may need very able people who can take a divergent view, their unstated need is for divergent views expressed in a convergent manner!

The level at which decisions are made about such interventions will vary. Coaching programmes may be deemed the property of HR to ensure the quality of delivery is not compromised. However, the story of effective talent management should not just be measured at corporate level or by the sponsorship of senior leaders. Consistent support matters – talent management needs to be understood at the top; a passing fad which is under-resourced and lacks direction or attempts to imitate the approach of other organisations is unlikely to succeed in the long run.

Arguably more significant to most employees is their line manager, who can potentially play a pivotal role as an ambassador and supporter of development. This is only going to work if they feel themselves to be a key player in the wider development process and accountable for the development of their team.

Employee engagement

A key driver of employee engagement is the connection employees perceive between the importance of their job and their consequent connection to the organisation. The characteristics of effective self-management are the very skills that managers can deploy to develop better connectedness between themselves and their teams. Yet all too often employee engagement initiatives fail to deliver what the organisation expects and employees anticipate. Death by a thousand questionnaires can produce employee disengagement through the absence of clear objectives and a structured approach to follow up and appropriate corrective action. However, the prize of delivering effective employee engagement is considerable: bringing the organisation closer together by creating a significant shift in behaviour delivering increased unity of purpose, improved motivation, greater customer focus, higher retention of key talent and better decision-making at all levels.

Those organisations and leaders that are effective have a number of key characteristics in common:

• They are output focused, rather than box tickers

• They take ownership of the programme, wishing to strategically embed employee engagement into their business

• They understand the need to challenge themselves on what they want and the effort they will need to make to get change to happen

- They take a joined-up perspective of delivery, acknowledging the role of line managers in the process

These benefits have never been more important as global uncertainty continues to create unexpected challenges for all employers. Tapping into the intrinsic talent of your workforce and strengthening a culture within which innovation can flourish are no longer optional, they are imperative. Furthermore the scale of the benefit to the organisation in retaining good people is frequently underestimated. It includes:

- The "churn" caused by a departure which may unsettle other colleagues and produce frictional costs in determining how best to respond to the departure

- The cost of finding a replacement, whether the internal opportunity costs or fees for recruiters, search firms and advertising

- Most significantly, the time it will take for a new employee to become effective.

Employee engagement is sometimes presented as a silver-bullet solution. The reality is quite the opposite; building active employee engagement processes that add value to the business requires an investment in time at the planning phase and openness to new approaches during implementation.

Oliver Hibbert, an employee engagement specialist with Nexus Consulting, comments that: "As paradigms change, the apparently ordered and static boundaries within organisations, departments and functions become more dynamic; merging and changing. All multinationals face the contrasting pulls of centralised company culture and diverse local cultures. The reality is that genuine engagement is strongly local, even in the biggest multinational. Mankind has for most of its history worked in small groups that met face to face and developed trust. Technology and economics have changed that only recently, and our innate sense of group is still face to face: like soldiers in battle, most people are most strongly aware of the people working near them, not of the wider organisation. Engagement is also essentially a combination of local pride and identity – it needs to be respected and encouraged. The sense of local identity is precious, and organisations need to grow it because much crucial knowledge and motivation is locked in local bits of the company – and in the case of acquisitions is a key part of the company value. But equally individuals need to get themselves heard and seen outside their immediate teams. If you want to develop your career, you need to be able to connect across the organisation so that others understand your value and the contribution that you bring."

Performance management and career development

Just as ambiguity over roles and boundaries causes tension and frustration, so can the absence of appropriate language to describe performance and potential. Do performance management processes actively advance superior performance is a question that cannot always be answered in the affirmative. The complexity of some of the processes can also get in the way of an open dialogue; the giveaway that things are not working is most obvious when an organisation's competency framework is not mandated as essential when a search firm is engaged. If not fit for this purpose, what is it useful for?

At its worst, the process may exhibit the following symptoms:

- There is a wide variation in how superior or poor performance is actually assessed, with hearsay rather than observation driving much of the process.

- Personal rather than objective judgements of performance and potential are allowed to go unchallenged.

- A willingness to suggest actions others need to take to improve performance is prevalent.

- There is no collective ownership of solutions, with senior manager accountability not clear.

- The feelings of both the appraiser and appraisee are not surfaced early enough and come to a head during the "performance interview."

Hopefully very few organisations have all of these characteristics! However, many organisations do have processes that are seen as a paper-based chore without which pay reviews will stall, rather than one of the means by which individuals will be encouraged to fulfil their potential. Such a process is also unlikely to surface performance issues at a stage when remedies may be available. This does both the organisation and the employee a disservice.

Turnarounds, mergers and acquisitions

This book has made frequent reference to change and uncertainty. Organisations "under duress" as they prepare for, or come to terms with the need for restructuring, merger or acquisition all have their own set of talent and career management issues.

Without effective processes and tools to measure individual potential and the barriers to optimising organisational performance, achieving the level of change required may move from challenging to insurmountable. Furthermore, individuals who may be critical to short-term success can fail to buy in to the need for a turnaround, or underestimate their own role in making the case for change. In the midst of considerable uncertainty and upheaval such behaviours are often not picked up as a major issue, effectively getting under the radar as an irritant rather than an obstacle.

There are a number of significant consequences:

- The wrong signals are sent to the people you really need

- The speed of execution may be slowed

- Precious time is eventually required to "sort out" people issues

- The frictional cost of inappropriate behaviour exerts a negative impact on the organisation's morale, capability and performance

At times such as this, roles, boundaries and egos all need managing! Appropriately focused executive development, assessment and coaching can potentially assist the process of integrating teams and key individuals. Adopting as transparent an approach as possible to both retention **and** separation issues is critical. In real life there are winners and losers; there is little point ignoring this. The need is to plan carefully for the future, linking communication and motivation strategies with the business plan and sharing as much information as possible as early as possible. The way in which people leave organisations has a powerful impact on those who remain, and are you prepared to embrace the notion of "good leavers", with appropriate terms for those who recognise the new culture is not for them?

Individuals making the "right" noises may not be the people to take the business forward; apparently reluctant embracers of the new vision may have much more to offer. Similarly, just as there is a need to focus on "key" people, the importance of getting the "best from the rest" through targeted motivation and communication through line managers matters too. "Stars" are important; although you need to be very certain who they are! Equally, enabling managers to get the best from their teams at a time of considerable pressure – and opportunity – does not happen without support and encouragement.

The potential role of ROM

As organisations are becoming more complex and having to become increasingly nimble, it is not surprising that boundaries and roles are more uncertain. Pressure on results and cost reduction may potentially stifle innovation and creativity and send mixed messages to the employees that are needed to help the organisation move forward. Under duress we will all return to our default behaviour, if only briefly. Underpinning this book is the need for employees to proactively manage their careers. However, it may be that a significant proportion will require a little assistance to take the first step!

If we turn the notion of **ROM** on its head and place the line manager in the position of the initiator of discussions with team members on career opportunities, the paradigm shifts. Were you to be invited by your line manager to jointly explore how the organisation matches up against your personal ambitions and how you see your career developing, what would be your reaction?

There will be mixed views:

- A moaners' charter

- A complete waste of time

- Impossible – we have no time

- It would require training programmes at a time when our budgets are severely constrained

- Great idea – won't be followed up though

- If my last company had done this, I probably would not have left them

Others will be concerned over the "real" intent of this proposal.

However, a dialogue-based intervention, proactively offered by the "organisation", has considerable potential benefit for both parties:

- It supports the employee engagement process in a cost-effective manner.

- Is a flexible response to different generational aspirations. Recent Ernst & Young research suggests that Gen Y (millennials) respondents (13%) were significantly more likely to rank promotions over Gen X (5%) and boomers (4%) who may have already achieved these career milestones.

- Additionally the "millennial" generation, currently in the age range 15-35, are well connected and used to "instant" responses. Their expectation of frequent job moves will require new approaches to maintain their engagement with the job

- Provides an avenue to complement other diversity initiatives

- May be the only means by which an employee feels able to show concern about their career trajectory

It would be naive to believe this suggestion would work in all organisations, yet in part this approach is working already. Many managers are responsive to requests from their people to discuss their future within the organisation. However, these conversations sometimes end amiably enough but with little focus on what needs to happen next. A line manager, who is alert to the need to surface career issues and the feelings they may generate early enough to provide an appropriate response, might be a rarity in your own organisation.

This may be down to a lack of training and support rather than disinterest. It could be argued that a good boss does this intuitively; my own experience indicates the desire of many team leaders and supervisors to do this, but many feel restricted by the absence of a structure within which to practise it. It is also difficult to take an initiative if your own manager has little time or interest in such a dialogue with you.

For this shift to occur, the parochial view which some managers attach to the career development of "their" people will need adjustment. This requires them to "let go", but also to be "let in" to discussions on the unit's succession plans and the potential opportunities available.

Inevitably the lack of any opportunity for a continuing and constructive dialogue about career opportunities will sometimes be the trigger that initiates a search for a new job elsewhere and, as a consequence, begins the process of disengaging. Yet the benefit of retaining a good employee for a few years longer has a significant economic payoff for the organisation and the benefit of potentially enhanced employability for the individual.

How?

The core of this approach is a dialogue based upon an invitation to discuss career ambitions using a Career CV as illustrated below. The intent of the discussion is to enable and empower a review of an individual's direction of travel, their likes and dislikes. It may also potentially explain – but not excuse – areas where performance may not be as expected. Moreover, an adult-to-adult conversation focused on the individual as a whole rather than a belated review of the last 12 months, creates the opportunity for a new level of understanding. There will be concerns to overcome; when was the last time a team member in your organisation discussed their CV with their boss? After all the CV is a document you use to get yourself a job somewhere else isn't it? Not necessarily, since a variation on the CV has the capacity to become a very useful document for exploring internal opportunities.

A number of themes, notably the reasons for moving on from previous roles and lessons learned, are likely to evoke a level of discussion that will be markedly different to the one that is played out in selection interviews. Here the focus is on understanding the rationale for the actions taken rather than an assessment of their appropriateness. Many managers inherit teams and are often oblivious to the longer-term career drivers of their people and the pattern of their career moves. This biographical look at an individual's progress and experience may trigger thoughts by both the manager and the individual about future roles which could potentially suit their skill set.

By discussing life before the current role – and organisation – a perspective can be gained on where the current job is located on their preferred career pathway. This gives both participants the opportunity to reflect on the "fit" with what may have been expected when joining/taking the job. Many of us, when asked to identify the most essential aspects of our job, deliver an answer that differs from that of our boss. Sometimes the difference is subtle, reflecting personal preferences, but the gap may be more significant. This may be related to organisational culture, operating style and team behaviour. Additionally, a discussion based on an exploration of "differences" rather than "failings" provides the opportunity to talk about the implications of this for future career moves.

The conversation also lends itself to the stage at which the employee currently sees their career inside the organisation. In terms of the steps used in this book, the start point has shifted to "demonstrating competence". In itself this typology shifts the focus of the discussion from "in or out" or loyalty to the organisation toward a more useful look at where the individual may actually feel themselves to be. For example, a newcomer to an organisation which has subsequently embarked on a major transformation may have concerns about the security of their employment. Someone with longer service may, for the first time, raise questions about their promotability and potential mobility. As an HR Director I had a conversation with such an individual who mentioned, in passing, their family connections with Asia. This subsequently led to a successful expatriate posting and a bigger job upon their return.

Steps

Issues and Concerns

Demonstrating competence	"It seems that the skills for which I was hired are not really valued here"
Arriving and delivering	"Having come from another sector I now realise my learning curve is going to be steeper than I thought"
Consolidating and reviewing	"It would be useful to get more regular feedback on how you feel I am performing"
Mapping	"I'm not sure there is an obvious next step for me here, especially given the hiring freeze"
Planning	"What development opportunities are there for me?"
Exploring	"In the spirit of openness you need to know I am looking elsewhere"

The dialogue-based approach supports the organisation's employee engagement processes, and in so doing surfaces issues that are going to show up in other ways if left unresolved.

Some of these issues may be down to misperception; the good news is the fact that they have surfaced. These may require resolution outside of this dialogue. These could include discussions on training needs, development opportunities, internal job opportunities in other functions or locations and, potentially, a move to another organisation. They may also focus on performance issues. As discussed earlier, this process complements the performance management process; it does not replace it.

Career CV Template

Name:	
It would be useful if you could describe the "Return on Myself" you are looking for from your employment here at XYZ:	
Career history - most recent first:	
Date of joining (organisation/college/university):	
Reasons for joining:	
Job title:	
Reporting to:	
Key responsibilities:	
Key achievements:	
Key learning:	
Date of leaving and reasons for moving on:	

Just as talent management may come to be perceived as the property of the corporate centre, the boundary management of this initiative matters. The principal dialogue will be between the individual and their direct boss or his/her line manager. Discussion on some of the outcomes which may emerge from the dialogue will require wider discussion, such as potential career moves in the future. However, the principal focus at the outset is grounded in the team environment in which the individual works. It has the potential to be an important bridge between both employee engagement and performance management enabling the participant's perspective on their career to be raised in a participative manner.

The protocols

- This is not a confidential process; of its very nature the line manager may need to work with HR to test out ideas on possible career moves

- It is important that the process is transparent, with clarity on the scope of meetings and an understanding that further discussions may be necessary

- Boundaries need to be clear too; the process is complementary to other initiatives – not a replacement for them

- Next steps: after each meeting, both parties need to reflect on what was discussed and agreed and jointly determine the actions that will follow and who has accountability for them

- Participation is voluntary

Issues to consider

- The level of discussion leader – direct boss or their line manager?

- The population within which the initiative will be rolled out – team, department or function?

- A pilot roll-out?

- Training and evaluation?

Training

Training line managers is best done in a workshop setting with participants working on their own CVs and practising with colleagues. Of itself this provides an opportunity for participants to reflect on their own expectations and to take stock of their own feelings about the future. This is also a useful means of re-engaging line managers with the organisation's talent and development process, refreshing their understanding of the working of talent pipelines and talent initiatives. This may raise more issues than anticipated and sufficient time needs to be taken to address concerns.

It is important to understand the boundaries within which such an approach sits and that it is complementary to other processes. The active involvement of HR is a prerequisite. The training outline below is based on developing an approach using coaching skills. This will both safeguard the process and also widen the line manager's people management repertoire and would typically include sessions on:

CONTEXT

- Reasons for the initiative
- Participant perspectives on the role of the line manager as:
  - Performance manager
  - Talent spotter
  - Career developer

INITIATION

- Organisational context

- Understanding the context, purpose and contracting with the participant

- Building appropriate relationships and creating appropriate terms of reference

BUILDING AND DELIVERING

- Communicating effectively: listening, questioning, reflecting

- Facilitating learning for the participant

- Providing feedback

- Understanding resistance

- Reviewing and utilising the knowledge generated

- Ending effectively

STRUCTURE

- Duration/frequency/outcomes

LINKING

- With function and HR/talent function

- Maintaining appropriate dialogue with the participant

The degree to which line managers see the benefits of this approach and feel themselves able to actively engage with it will be telling. How clearly they perceive themselves as playing a role as performance manager, talent spotter and career developer is a key issue. There is a potential win/win for all parties in moving in this direction but in some organisations the positioning will need to be undertaken with care. This will be particularly important in organisations which have successively delayered their management ranks, where demotivated indi-viduals may, for a variety of reasons, be acting as blockers rather than enablers. Yet if this is the case, your employee engagement initiatives are already at risk.

Of itself this initiative may not make an immediate difference. However, in the longer term an increase in the retention of key talent and the creation of a culture which encourages transparent discussions on career potential are significant benefits for any organisation.

The Takeaway

ROM has importance for the individual and can also help the organisation reframe the dialogue around promotability and performance. The organisational role of line manager as performance manager, talent spotter and career developer also merits further consideration.

Chapter Twelve
Taking Stock

> "We should not judge people by their peak of excellence; but by the distance they have travelled from the point where they started."

Henry Ward Beecher

This book has covered a number of themes. Their resonance will depend on a variety of factors, not least the specific needs of each particular reader. In some cases the text may have been a wake-up call, in others a confirmation that your approach to managing your career is on the right lines. Many people under-estimate the progress they have made. You don't need to compare yourself with others to do this. Consider where you started and where you see yourself now. Revisiting the matrix below will help you to do this and may also give you the impetus to offer help to others whether as a mentor or provider of feedback.

As a team leader you may wish to engage your colleagues in using the CV-based approach to career dialogue.

In any event, please take a moment to note down the actions that you will now be taking to self-manage your career and the support you will be giving colleagues and team members to do the same.

In the spirit of self-management, this book does not contain a list of addresses and organisations; there are two appendices which look at the basics of interviews and an exploration of how to connect with your feelings when making decisions.

Steps

		Current level of understanding 0=low/10=high	Current level of effectiveness 0=low/10=high
STEPS			
Mapping	How well do I understand my current situation?		
Planning	What next – the potential options and resources required		
Exploring	How aware am I of the opportunities available to me? Testing out opportunities		
Demonstrating competence	Does my CV and interview technique currently support my strengths, ambitions and the needs of potential employers?		
Arriving and delivering	What needs to be done to make a difference early in a new role		
Consolidating and reviewing	How will I enhance my reputation in the new organisation and maintain a longer-term focus?		
SELF-MANAGEMENT			
Balancing focus and desire	Ensuring a balanced approach to targeting the right jobs for the right reasons		
Insight	How self-aware am I? How well do I understand how others perceive me? What opportunities are available to me?		
Connecting	Spotting the opportunities that match my goals at the right time. How good a networker am I?		

PROCESSES			
Feedback and the Performance Review	Recent feedback from peers and others? How well do I understand my organisation's Performance Review Process?		
Outplacement, executive coaching and mentoring	How well do I understand these processes and the benefits they might provide?		
My Big Fat CV	Do I have a "master" CV that supports my understanding of my career drivers and ambitions and demonstrates my competence?		

The Takeaway

The best resource you have is yourself! So use your draft plan to get started and remember STAN (Safe To Admit Need)!

Good luck!

Appendix A
Moving Forward: Interview 101

In the context of the self-management characteristics discussed earlier, insight and outsight are particularly relevant to becoming effective at interviews. This will underpin your preparation, which should be based on gaining as good an understanding as you can of both the role and organisation that has the job you are hoping to get. Balancing focus and desire will ensure that you listen to the questions and provide clear, structured answers along with enthusiasm for the opportunity the role will offer. Finally, your connections may be a good source of people with whom you can do a dry run or two to get feedback on the authenticity of your reasons for applying and the skills and experience you will bring.

The most visible aspect of the selection process is the interview. For some jobs there may only be one interview; for others there may be a number of interviews with the HR department, the person you would be working for, and the people you might be working with. The more senior the role, the more likely the process is to include key stakeholders, including NEDs.

At its most straightforward, an interview is a conversation with a purpose to find out whether you are the right person for the job in terms of:

• Your ability to do the job – capability

• Your motivation to do the job well – capacity

- Whether you will fit in with the rest of the team

- Gathering evidence on what you actually do rather than what you say you do and, in so doing, benchmarking your competence (knowledge, skills and behaviour) against the demands of the job

The interviewer will typically want to:

- Get you to do most of the talking

- Get you to expand on relevant experience

- Get accurate information on what you've done and how you did it

- Explore how you see your career developing

- Examine the rationale for your application

They will do this by:

- Asking questions

- Observing your responses

- Determining your suitability using psychometric or skills-related assessments

Preparing for the interview involves a range of activities:

- Ensuring you have as much information as possible on the job and your potential future employer

- Mapping out what you think is going to be asked

- Putting yourself in the place of your interviewer and reflecting on what you would ask if you were in their shoes

- Practising your responses to the questions you may be asked

- Ensuring you know what you will ask to get as full a picture as possible of the role and the reward package

Everyone will benefit from doing this; it's a bit like an MOT, without which you may not do yourself justice. Remember it's not just your answers but your demeanour during an interview which is subject to scrutiny. It's not just what we say, but how we look when we speak and how we present ourselves. For example, minimal eye contact can create an impression of disinterest or lack of confidence and long-winded, rambling answers will leave a negative impression which gets remembered. "Underprepared and unaware" was the way I overheard a candidate described in a coffee bar recently.

It may be that you are about to visit a recruiter for an initial discussion on your experience and ambitions and whether they may be able to help you. In reality this is an interview rather than a discussion, so stay focused! Here are some of the questions you are likely to be asked:

- Tell us about yourself

- Describe your ideal job

- Describe your management style

- How would your team describe you?

- How would you rate yourself as a team player?

- Tell me about the best job you've had

- Who made the biggest impact on your career?

- What are you looking for in your next job?

- Tell us more about the career moves you have made

- How satisfied are you with the outcomes?

- What else should we have asked you?

Anticipating the types and depth of questions you will be asked will be related to the seniority of the role, but everyone should expect to be asked about their experience, expectations and achievements covering such themes as:

- How you rate yourself as a team player

- Working with others

- Leading and managing people

- Getting results

- Getting the detail right

- Communication

- Handling change

- Customer or client service

- Delegation and time management

- Setting priorities

More senior roles are likely to address some or all of the themes below which focus on the need to manage change and develop strategic response to uncertain market conditions:

- Coping with whatever challenges currently present themselves

- Building and defining a range of futures that the organisation could face

- Crafting solutions to manage uncertainty

- Managing the processes required to respond to the need for change

- Leading the strategic repositioning of the organisation

You should develop your own responses to these questions.

Whilst the job description for the role you are applying for is the most useful for anticipating the questions you are likely to encounter, remember that a range of wider themes will be explored. These will invariably include:

- Your motivation for applying for this job

- The way your career has evolved

A range of potential interview questions are set out below. Not all of these will be relevant to your own circumstances, but they do provide the basis for understanding the themes that a recruiter or search firm will focus on and can be adapted for your own use:

Q) What would your ideal boss behave like?

Q) Who's your best leadership role model?

Q) Give us some examples of situations where you've had to really enthuse your team to go the extra mile. What were your inputs and what were the outcomes?

Q) When you are under pressure, how do you feel people perceive you?

Q) What do you see as the biggest personal stretch for you in this role?

Q) What do you think makes a team stand out from the rest? How well do the teams you've managed stand up against these criteria?

Q) What do you perceive to be the most significant challenges facing XYZ?

Q) Take us through the most difficult business decision you've had to make so far in your career.

Q) Reflecting on the most complex project you've been involved with, outline the key lessons you have learned.

Q) If you were us, what would you expect to be achieved during your first year in the role?

Q) If you're having a bad day at the office, how do others see you?

Q) This role will require someone who is resilient in the face of market and organisational pressures. Give us some examples of your own resilience.

Q) Take us through your approach to influencing your peers to see things your way.

Q) What will be your key priorities/potential actions during the first three months in this role?

Q) What do you see as the key requirements to creating a team where excellence is the norm?

Q) How do you deal with poor performance?

Q) What's been the biggest surprise in your current role?

Q) How will you measure success after 12 months in the job? How do you feel we should assess success?

Q) What is your ideal working relationship with a boss?

Q) What makes you the right person for this job?

Q) Take us through your most difficult career decision

Q) How would your current boss describe you?

Q) Give us an example of a time when you have gone the extra mile to support one of your colleagues.

Q) Have there been times during your career when you feel, on reflection, that your actions may have been counterproductive?

Q) When you're not sure of the next step, what do you do?

Q) In our business we have people with substantial experience, strong egos and a track record of delivery. How will you persuade them that your course of action is the right one?

Q) What behaviours won't you tolerate as a boss?

Q) How do you currently seek feedback on your performance? What difference has this made?

Q) What do you think it will take to grow a high performing team for XYZ? What qualities will you look for in your direct reports?

Q) If your direct reports were with us today, what would they say they wanted more of/less of from you as a boss?

Q) How do you expect to balance the challenge of building a bigger business with day-to-day delivery issues?

Q) What would a neutral observer see as your greatest strength and your most pressing development need?

Simply running through your answers to these questions in your head is not going to prove very useful. To help yourself you need to:

- Revisit MBFCV; this is an invaluable preparatory tool. Also re-read the CV you are using for this application

- Articulate your proposed response to the question

- Write this down and reflect upon your answer

- Practise actually giving the answer again

- Ideally get someone to help you by acting as the "interviewer", or tape your responses

- If you have a helper, get them to rate the factors in the observation box below to get some feedback or use this as your own aide-memoire

- Reflect on whether your answers actually answered the question!

What did you see and hear?

Rate this as very good, good, average, poor and very poor and explain why:

- Eye contact?
- Clear answers?
- Addressed the question?
- Avoided the question?
- Came across in an engaging manner?
- Appeared focused?
- Well prepared?
- Provided credible examples of experience?
- Made good use of the time available?
- Appeared unflustered?
- Worth seeing again?

Building on this is the opportunity to focus on the questions you would really rather not be asked! By now there may be very few of these. Reflecting on what you really do not want to be asked is important. What underpins your concern? It is best to be truthful; desire can overtake focus leading to poor decisions. This involves accepting equal responsibility for the choices you have made.

Repeated below is a reminder of the themes explored in Chapter Eight:

- **Language.** Is your career story plausible, are reverses explained, and are your responses to questions indicative of empathy with the needs of the role you would be moving into?

- **Patterns.** Frequent moves or no moves at all require explanation and context. Successively bigger roles in one organisation or regular moves based on being headhunted?

- **Cause and effect.** Did you move or were you pushed? What was the difference you personally made? As noted earlier, you may feel you are currently working for the organisation from hell; expect to be questioned on what led you to move there in the first place and what this may signal about your judgement.

- **Trajectory.** Ever upward with no blips or a phased progression based on seeking appropriate opportunities? Have you reached your ceiling? Or are you someone who moves on "just in time"?

- **Understanding.** What are the lessons you have learned and the impact of this learning upon your approach to managing and leading? Learning from failure can be a key asset.

- **Rationale.** Why the interest in this role at this time?

- **The narrative/story.** Taken as a whole, do you succeed in demonstrating your credibility as someone worthy of consideration for this or other roles? It could be that you trigger a thought on the part of the search firm about your suitability for assignments they are conducting for other clients.

It is all too easy to become so focused on the questions you may be asked at the expense of other basic but essential tasks. At the very basic end of the scale is getting oneself to the right place on the right day in the right frame of mind. So make sure you:

- Don't arrive late!

- Treat everyone you meet with courtesy

- Look – listen – learn

- Be clear – don't mumble

- Don't talk too much

- Maintain interest – and eye contact

- Think carefully about describing your current situation

- Be honest

- Take a spare CV

At the end of the interview, ask the interviewer how they see you matching the job requirements. You may get the response that it's early days in the process and you will need to be patient, so also ensure you understand the next step and when you are likely to hear anything. If you have got the interview through a recruiter or search firm they will be the people who will update you, so let them know how you feel the interview went.

Although some people do succeed with their first application, many more do not, so track and record your feelings of each and every interview.

The information you need is:

- Date of interview

- Organisation

- Vacancy

- Interviewer(s)

- How do you feel the interview went?

- Summarise what you were told about the job and the organisation

- Do you believe you gave a good account of yourself?

- Any surprises?

- Any problems?

- Questions you wish you had anticipated?

- At this stage, do you have enough information to make up your mind?

- What happens next?

- Timescale?

Handling rejection

- The best person doesn't always get the job

- Rejection can be depressing for all of us – however, getting the wrong job for the wrong reasons can be much more harmful in the long run

- Don't take it personally – ask yourself if you would have given yourself the job

- Ask for feedback from the organisation

- Learn from your experience

Appendix B
At the Heart of Making a Decision

"Your visions will become clear only when you look into your heart. Who looks outside, dreams. Who looks inside, awakens."

Carl Jung

Effective career management requires a range of decisions to be made, sometimes very quickly and potentially with inadequate information. With this in mind, here is a perspective on connecting with your own feelings when confronted with making decisions. Many people refer to their "gut instinct" or relying on "my intuition" and, in this personal reflection, Tim Johnson* explores this:

Making decisions – good or poor, big or small – is something we do all the time. For senior executives making the "right" decision is crucial to a business in terms of its future performance and even its continued existence. Yet executives these days are increasingly faced with situations where there is no clear premise on which to base decisions. No longer can we just rely on past statistics, experience or know-how to provide us with predictions for the future, accurate or otherwise. The world isn't like that anymore. Businesses are ever more moving into uncharted territories that require decisions outside the realm of what was known before. How then do we make decisions that are neither limited (because we don't yet have the information) nor just "gut instinct" or "intuition"? How can we ensure the decisions we are indeed making are the best ones, which also take account of things that have not yet manifested or become obvious to us?

Whether it is a simple choice or a genuinely more complex decision such as whether to change career direction, we are generally thrown back onto well-tested methodologies. We rely on a mix of assessing external factors, past experience, expected outcomes and what we loosely call "gut feeling". Time will tell us whether we made a "good" or "bad" decision. Sometimes we are not 100% honest with ourselves. It is not uncommon to try to shoehorn the eventual outcome into what we might have pretended we expected.

However, what if there were another way, a way that relies on being able to access a much deeper truth and a way that can move us away from our useful but not always totally accurate gut feeling? There is. It is called opening your heart and through this we can then access the Truth from within the core of our heart, known as our Inner Heart. Centered within the Inner Heart is an Inner Wisdom that transcends the mind, the limitations of our human-based knowledge and our ego. It is this knowledge that we can all tap into once we have learnt a few simple techniques.

When I first started running a successful executive search business, providing specialist senior level recruitment solutions to the highly focused international insurance and reinsurance world, I had not discovered how to access my heart and Inner Heart, concepts that will be described later. Yet later development of this soft skill proved inordinately useful in speeding up the search process for "C" suite and senior technical, operational and functional executive level posts. This also became beneficial to the client with improved selection decisions.

Of course, even in using the Inner Heart for guidance it is still necessary for the search consultant to have professional networks to be able to convey the nature and scope of the position to other professionals from the same or similar fields who will understand what is being sought. However, at an early stage when exploring the potential universe from where candidates might be sourced, I found the Inner Heart was able to give direction on the best companies or areas of the market where the most suited candidates might be found. It should be remembered that you could not literally go through a list with a pin and wait to feel for a positive response. When an approach is made to potentially interested individuals, they will have their own agendas, choices and free will at play and, while they may indeed technically be the best candidate, they may simply not want to move positions at that stage in their lives.

When it comes to interviewing possible candidates before they are presented to the client, most search consultants will tell you that gut feel or instinct will give a strong indicator who should go forward. Whilst I too used to rely on this, I now find accessing the 'truth' from within my heart enables me to know instantly if a prospective candidate is saying the truth or overstating about their abilities; or to make clearer selection decisions, even in the apparent face of contradictory evidence. For example, a few years ago I interviewed what appeared to be a highly introverted candidate for a sales management role, a quality that would not have been right for the position. My instinct was to place him right at the bottom of the shortlist. However, my Inner Heart gave a strong positive response to the candidate's suitability so I persevered when usual reactions would have been to draw the interview to an earlier close.

After further investigation into his career, he began to open up much more to the extent that he felt able to confide what had recently happened in his life. Two days before our meeting day, a tragic accident had happened within his immediate circle of friends. He was clearly trying to come to terms with the impact of this but he had not wanted this to be brought into the interview environment as he felt this would have been unprofessional. This led to a much more meaningful and frank discussion. He went on to become the candidate selected by the client for the position.

So what is this heart connection I am referring to?

Let's be clear here. I am not talking about the physical heart that tirelessly circulates blood around the body, although even this has a capacity and power that is now proven to be well beyond that of the brain. Rather, I am referring to our non-physical (spiritual) heart. If you are uncomfortable with that term think of this as being the centre where you feel joy and happiness. Imagine seeing a baby smile and giggle, maybe a kitten or puppy playing without a care in the world or perhaps that soft gentle feeling in the chest when we first fell in love or when we meet an old friend again after many years apart. Those thoughts or recollections will produce a "warm" or "sweet" feeling in the centre of your chest. That feeling is not coming from a physical organ but from your spiritual, non-physical heart. The good news is everybody has a "spiritual" heart as well as a physical heart, even if for many it may seem that such pleasant, light feelings are but a dim and distant reminder of a time long ago. Life brings many knocks and disappointments. Without a strong connection to our heart these can eventually become overwhelming and burden us with cynicism, negativity, depression or even worse cause untold pain for us, our friends, families and colleagues.

Of course we use the word heart in many common expressions: a heartfelt welcome, speaking from the heart, a kind-hearted person or even, on a more negative note, hard hearted. Writers from most cultures refer to the heart, particularly in love poetry. The following selection of quotations mentioning the heart shows a breadth of time and cultures:

> *"The best and most beautiful things in the world cannot be seen or even touched. They must be felt with the heart."*

Helen Keller

> *"One learns through the heart, not the eyes or the intellect."*

Mark Twain

> *"Wherever you go, go with all your heart."*

Confucius

> *"Few are those who see with their own eyes and feel with their own hearts."*

Albert Einstein

> *"Educating the mind without educating the heart is no education at all."*

Aristotle

It is interesting to note that Aristotle, writing 23 centuries ago, identifies a heart education as being just as important as a mind or head education. However, certainly in the UK education curriculum, the heart does not appear currently to feature even remotely.

So what exactly is the heart, how can we access it, and how can this help us to make decisions?

It is well recognised (in Chinese, Indian and other Eastern traditions and many healing modalities) that a human has seven major chakras. One of those chakras is known as the heart chakra. Our non-physical, spiritual heart is located inside this heart chakra. A chakra – the word derives from the Sanskrit word meaning a wheel or circle – is an energy centre connected to organs of the body. For example the heart chakra is connected to the physical heart as well as the lungs and lymph glands. However, chakras are also connected to aspects of our emotional and mental well-being.

Within our non-physical heart we have our Inner Heart and at the core of this, our spirit connection to The Source of All That Is. Let's call this True Source. Many ancient spiritual books stated that the biggest secret lies in the core of our heart and that is our Inner Heart, heart of the heart, which always knows the truth and always directs us to True Source, the source of our truest self.

Let us just pause here for a moment. Particularly here in the secular Western world we may often baulk at such language as this, dismissing discussion of non-physical energies and True Source as being on the lunatic fringe. Some may also associate such language with religious dogma and instantly switch off so that we ignore rather than allow ourselves to examine. But once again, remember that we can all feel that warm/sweet/gentle sensation of our heart reacting to a baby's smile as mentioned above. That feeling is coming from somewhere. And it is not the brain. Let us just call that True Source, but you may replace that with any term you apply if you have a belief in a creator.

Up until 2006, I too would have considered talk of the heart and chakras etc. as at best mumbo jumbo. I started to read about alternative healing methodologies, as conventional medicine had nothing to offer me when I was suffering with burnout. Through this I discovered Reiki and later I uncovered some-thing called Reiki Tummo. The steps are so easy to learn. You touch your heart with one or two fingers at a point that is on your sternum at the height of your armpits. You smile. That sweet or gentle feeling, mentioned before, will be there and that is the start of our connection to True Source. You then follow that feeling without looking for it or trying to hold onto it. It is truly that simple.

Except for a few necessary pieces of detailed information and a theoretical overview, which anybody can understand, opening the heart, the first stage to accessing the wisdom within the Inner Heart, happens easily through structured practices. These begin with feeling the heart, progressing to opening the heart and then being able to enjoy being in the heart for longer peri-ods so that the heart begins to be able to be connected to True Source for longer.

The next stage in the process is to be connected to your Inner Heart and allowing this, the centre of truth, to become the dir-ector of your heart. Once this connection is established, your ability to make correct decisions increases dramatically.

The only feasible difficulty with opening the heart is the doubt that it can be quite so simple. Over thousands of years we have seen ever more complicated concepts and methods which have made it difficult for people to fix on to the real connection back to their source. We tend to believe that only a few famous enlightened people or saints have managed to achieve the state of perfection which most of us can only dream of.

But, you may ask, what does this have to do with making decisions?

For ages it has been said we should follow our heart, that our heart knows the truth. Why? This is because our truest self, the spark of True Source within our Inner Heart, has its own consciousness. This consciousness is much higher than our brain consciousness, and it knows the real truth – what is best for us and for others. As soon as we are able to use our heart properly, we can realise truths from within our own heart are better than "truths" from our limited brain. Often, these latter "truths" are not truths at all, but what we later find are mistakes based on limited or false information, flawed judgments or poor reasoning.

Within our Inner Heart is the spark of our True Source. It is always pure and cannot be contaminated by anything. There is a special layer that protects our Inner Heart from any outside impurity influences. So, when you connect to your Inner Heart you are being connected to True Source and thus to the Source of Truth. Does this sound rather too good to be true?

What becomes a problem is that most people's Inner Hearts are closed because their hearts are not open yet. With a closed heart, one's Inner Heart cannot function at all. This means that the wisdom that resides within is not being used in our daily lives. Even a criminal has an Inner Heart, though it is clear from his/her actions that the Inner Heart does not function at all. However, as soon as that person uses his/her Inner Heart and makes decisions based on the wisdom from the heart then, at that moment, he/she is directing him/herself to True Source.

This shows how important and astonishing the power of the Inner Heart is.

It is not enough to simply know about your Inner Heart. As my teacher on opening the heart, Irmansyah Effendi (Irman for short) has said on a number of occasions: "There are so many good things about the heart. However, knowing and talking about it are not enough. To gain all of its benefits, we have to use it properly." Through guided practices you can be helped to learn very effective techniques to help you open and strengthen your heart and activate your Inner Heart, so your Inner Heart becomes stronger and is continuously able to direct your whole self and your whole life to True Source.

Practice really does make perfect as you begin to trust the responses you receive even to matters where you have no brain idea. Recently I asked my heart to show me how my physical body reacts to different kinds of milk: cow's milk – full fat or semi-skimmed, almond milk, rice milk, oat milk and even hemp milk which seems to have recently appeared in my local supermarket. In my particular case, oat milk produced a much more settled and gentle feeling in my heart than the others although none were really bad – so now oat milk is what I use on breakfast cereal.

The heart will always give you the best answer, the real truth if you will. Be warned, this may not be what you want or were expecting to hear. Should we work with that new client who seems so keen to offer us a big contract? Your brain and all the figures and spreadsheets are saying yes but the heart is indicating no. Well maybe there are factors that have been overlooked or that are outside of what you have been able to discover. This can be a very difficult decision to broker to other members of your team, as they will probably not be sympathetic to or supportive of heart decisions to begin with. Of course we exercise free will so there is nothing to stop you physically from pursuing the course your brain has decided. However, wait and see what the consequences are if the heart feedback is ignored.

Be assured the heart is never wrong. However, you cannot use it for selfish economic gain or to extract unfair competitive advantage. Do not expect to be able to get next Saturday's lottery numbers either unless this was genuinely going to benefit you. For most lottery winners this is not the case. The heart will present you with the best decision all round for all parties, the decision you would make if you could be in possession of all material facts and the consequences thereof, something which you will never be able to achieve in normal circumstances.

Nothing is set in stone and so it is possible to receive what may appear to be contradictory advice from the heart over a period of time. This will usually be because in the meantime we may have taken certain steps so that the circumstances have changed. Remember, we have free will and our lives are not prescribed.

How does the feeling from the heart differ from intuition or gut feeling? At a simple level the gut is beneath the heart so the feelings will emanate from different points. Gut feeling is associated with our solar plexus chakra where fears tend to be stored and therefore decisions taken by reference to this area will more often than not be based on fear. This may be very useful when making a snap – almost animalistic – decision about whether we like or trust somebody who we may suddenly be confronted with, but it is no substitute for proper heart connection.

We should always use our Inner Heart in making important decisions. Let us not forget the brain though. The brain is a fabulous instrument that, as we know, is scarcely understood by the medical world. In making those everyday decisions such as weighing up sensory information about crossing the road or deciding what time to leave the office to get to an external meeting it is probably not necessary to check out with the heart. However, if it is a decision whether it is worthwhile to attend that meeting in the first place, then the Inner Heart will give the best guidance. Establishing a healthy relationship between our brain and heart is vitally important. Our heart, when connected to True Source, should be what leads our brain and actions, not vice versa. Our gut instinct is, as mentioned before, often driven from fear so will not lead us to the best outcomes.

Opening the heart has many benefits that go way beyond decision-making. Being calmer, healthier, more relaxed, less ego-centered and happier are but a few of the advantages we gain. Using our heart is the start of a beautiful journey. It will make decision-making easier, less stressful and more productive. It will certainly help to reduce the level of our own will in making decisions that are not good for us and others and it will connect you to the Source you have been searching for, possibly without your even knowing it, for a very long time. It will build your trust in the Source and, through this, the trust you can have in your own decisions.

In my old business of executive search and indeed most other industries, it is well recognised that cognitive intelligence and emotional intelligence are key characteristics required of any successful senior executive. What have invariably been overlooked are the skills necessary to access the innate wisdom and intelligence of the Inner Heart, mainly because these have simply not been acknowledged and taught before. It is these that inform good decision-making and will increasingly differentiate truly great companies from their competitors as we move into progressively more uncharted economic waters.

My thanks go to a fellow heart student, Jacqui Gascoyne, for her support and contribution to this work.

For fuller information about how to open your heart, please refer to: *http://www.padmacahaya.org*

* Tim Johnson has spent the majority of his career in the global insurance and reinsurance markets as a technician, business developer and manager, subsequently co-founding an executive search firm targeted at the insurance industry.